RETAIL 101

The Guide to Managing and Marketing
Your Retail Business

NICOLE L. REYHLE

and

JASON A. PRESCOTT

New York   Chicago   San Francisco   Athens   London   Madrid
Mexico City   Milan   New Delhi   Singapore   Sydney   Toronto

1 2 3 4 5 6 7 8 9 0 DOC/DOC 1 0 9 8 7 6 5 4

ISBN 978-0-07-184014-9
MHID 0-07-184014-1

e-ISBN 978-0-07-184015-6
e-MHID 0-07-184015-X

Library of Congress Cataloging-in-Publication Data

Reyhle, Nicole.
  Retail 101 : the guide to managing and marketing your retail business / by Nicole Reyhle and Jason Prescott.
    pages cm
  ISBN 978-0-07-184014-9 (alk. paper) — ISBN 0-07-184014-1 (alk. paper) 1. Retail trade—Management. 2. Marketing. I. Prescott, Jason. II. Title.
  HF5429.R488 2014
  658.8'7—dc23   2014008760

McGraw-Hill Education books are available at special quantity discounts to use as premiums and sales promotions or for use in corporate training programs. To contact a representative, please visit the Contact Us pages at www .mhprofessional.com.

To my husband, Eric: You are the best partner in every way. We can do anything when we do it together, and I'm most grateful for what we've already created— Claire and Jackson.

To my parents: Mom, you are my best friend, and I admire you very much. And Dad, knowing you are watching over us from above is both comforting and bittersweet.

I love you all so much.

—Nicole Leinbach Reyhle

To my future wife, Dominique: Your six years of support have given definition to the journey. I can't wait to dedicate the next one to *My Wife*. I love, thank you, and feel alive every day with you by my side.

—Jason A. Prescott

Contents

Acknowledgments   ix

Introduction   xiii

Part I: Being Indie in a Big-Box World   1

1 • Standing Out among the Crowd   3
   Action Guide   6

2 • Stepping Outside Your Comfort Zone   9
   Habits of Successful Retailers   14
   Action Guide   19

3 • Leaning on Outside Organizations   21
   Getting Involved with Outside Organizations   22
   Benefits That Organizations May Offer   29
   Action Guide   33

4 • Identifying Your Unique Store Story   39
   Creating an Inventory Assortment That Stands Out   41
   Unique Traits of Your Store   44
   General Interview Questions for Potential Employees   51
   Action Guide   55

Part II: Practical Steps to Increase Your Store Visibility and Sales

5 • Sourcing Products Through Trade Shows and the Internet   61

Benefits of Sourcing as a Retailer   62

Working with Wholesalers   70

Understanding the Value of Trade Shows   72

Managing Orders Placed at Shows   77

Using Online Sourcing Platforms   80

Action Guide   86

6 • Buying for Customers Versus Yourself   89

Understanding the Basics of Retail Math   90

Introducing Customer Feedback for Inventory Management   95

Using Point-of-Sale Software to Help Manage Inventory   99

Action Guide   102

7 • Selling Your Products   107

Introducing and Managing Store Events   108

Highlighting Inventory Through Displays   117

Using Modern Technology in Your Store   123

Identifying Whether Mobile Commerce Matters   126

Action Guide   128

8 • Applying Press and Marketing to Your Business   133

Using E-mail to Communicate Store Messages   141

Using the Internet as a Marketing Platform   144

Resources Every Independent Retailer Should Know About   146

Action Guide   148

Part III: Making a Mark in the Economy 151

9 • Making Your Presence Online   153

   Embracing E-commerce   154

   Social Media in Today's Retail Marketplace   164

   Action Guide   175

10 • Taking Part in Shop-Local Initiatives   177

   Understanding Buy-Local Campaigns   178

   Finding Success Through Small-Business Saturday   183

   Introducing Commerce and Charity   185

   Action Guide   186

11 • A Crystal Ball for Independent Retailers   189

   The Future of Independent Retail   190

   The Future Beyond Technology   194

   When Retail Isn't in Your Future   197

   Parting Words from Jason Prescott   200

   Parting Words from Nicole Leinbach Reyhle   202

   Conclusion   203

Appendix A: Resources for Independent Retailers   205

Appendix B: Common Retail Terms and Definitions   219

Notes   237

Index   243

Acknowledgments

Nicole Leinbach Reyhle

FIRST AND foremost, thank you to Jason Prescott for being such a great believer and supporter of Retail Minded and myself since day one. You were among the first industry leaders to reach out and work with me as a retail resource, and I'm grateful for our continued support of each other over the years. Furthermore, I can't thank you enough for the opportunity to coauthor this book together. Your wisdom, energy, and experience are invaluable.

Next, I want to extend a huge, general thank you to all the businesses, organizations, and people who contributed content and research material to this book. Jason and I both are very grateful for the insight, time, energy, and experience that you all provided. Without your support, this book simply would not be possible. Thank you again, and we wish each of you continued success in the future.

Next, I want to thank the people who were involved in the literal creation of this book. To start, Bill Gladstone, thank you. I appreciate your taking a chance on a first-time author and look forward to working with you much more in the future. Also, Tara Gladstone, thank you for your wisdom and support in creating the book proposal. While I had hoped to work with you more, our limited work together taught me so much, and I look forward to the chance to work with you again. Last, but certainly not least, thank you Thomas Miller, our editor at McGraw-Hill. Your guidance and enthusiasm throughout this project have been fantastic, and Jason and I both are grateful for your overall support. Dannalie Diaz from McGraw-Hill, I also appreciate your taking the time to give me some extra first-time author coaching as well.

Finally, I want to extend special thanks to some key contributors and supporters of this book. While there are too many to highlight, the following people went above and beyond to really help make this book the best it could be.

Suzy Teele, COO of SnapRetail, thank you. Your constant support is truly appreciated. Courtney Symons, marketing manager with Shopify, thank you for digging and searching for all the exact details we needed to make this book come to life. Camille Candella, group marketing director for Emerald Expositions, thank you for sharing your wisdom and helping retailers to better succeed. Jeff Milchen, codirector of the American Independent Business Alliance, thank for your invaluable insight and expertise. Don Davis, editor in chief at *Internet Retailer Magazine*, I appreciate your taking the time to share your unique perspectives and am grateful to offer them to our readers. Joe Abraham, author of *Entrepreneurial DNA* and CEO of Bosi DNA, I have been fortunate to work with you firsthand in my own business growth and am thrilled that you shared your wisdom with the readers of this book as well.

An additional thank you goes to all my Retail Minded partners, who helped to provide their expertise and insight to our readers, including Jeff Buehler of Main Street New Jersey; Andy Ellen and Christie Burris of North Carolina Retail Merchants Association;

Ellen Divita of the City of Geneva, Illinois; Lynne Schwartz of Downtown St. Charles Partnership; and Jama Rice of the Museum Store Association.

I'd like also to thank three folks I'm lucky to call my friends who also work with independent retailers as consultants, experts, and leaders. Georganne Bender and Rich Kizer, I've admired your work since we first met at the Dance Retailer Expo in Las Vegas many summers ago. I was lucky to learn that our offices were only a town apart, and since then, I'm grateful for our many lunches, brainstorming sessions, chitchats, and constant support that you have provided. Looking forward to our continued support and work with each other! In addition, a big thank you to Cathy Wagner. You're retail insight and friendship is very much appreciated. Finally, thank you to my family and friends. Being surrounded by good company at work, at home, and at play is a great way to live life, and I'm fortunate to do just that. Thank you.

Jason A. Prescott

I have always been a believer that one of the leading causes of success is passion. Nicole Reyhle, you are one of the most passionate professionals with whom I've ever had the honor of working. Thank you for the countless hours of research, interviews, and detail you brought to this book. You have a very special gift that is going to be responsible for the success of so many entrepreneurs and small-business owners. Your honesty, integrity, and professionalism will make you HIP for many years to come. It was my honor to help open the door, and I await with excitement our next project together.

Bill Gladstone, thank you for continuing to open your door. I never would have thought that we would be publishing not just one but two major business titles in under one year. You are a man of miracles, and I salute the belief you continue to have in all we accomplish together.

To Alain Stambouli, president of Via Trading, there are not very many people capable of emulating the success your company has had over the years. You continue to set the bar in a very dynamic industry, and I have no doubt that the trend will continue. Your business creates opportunities for thousands of retailers and powers an economic backbone for countless lives. As the Via Trading story continues, I'll always consider myself fortunate to have inspiring friends like you in my life.

And finally, I'd like to acknowledge all my friends, colleagues, customers, and partners who continue to be the propellers and motivators of every accomplishment I've been part of since 2005. My passion comes from you, and the path we continue down together has been an unforgettable and humbling experience. Serving you is a privilege, and I am eternally thankful for such an opportunity.

Introduction

I'D LIKE to believe that my career in retail never really began but rather always existed. As a little girl, I remember weaving in and out of stores with my mother and two sisters, always on the hunt for something for one of us. My mom—a competitive shopper who knew of every sale, new store opening, and special promotion that would be taking place—considered shopping more of a pastime than a responsibility. I, on the other hand, enjoyed our shopping experiences for much different reasons. Instead of being excited over a new top or some shoes, I would gravitate to the checkout area and try to chat with one of the sales associates about working in retail. Naturally, coming from a preteen, this conversation didn't go very far. However, by the time I was able to get my first part-time job, I knew that I wanted it to be in the retail world. Over the following years from ages 15 to 22, I worked at Things Remembered, The Limited, Ralph Lauren, Nordstrom, Max Studio, and ultimately, a little boutique in downtown Chicago called Chasalla. It was during that experience that I knew I wanted to somehow, someday support independent retailers. First, however, I knew that I needed a more expansive understanding of the dynamic world of retail.

The following years took me on a whirlwind tour of both retail and wholesale. My first job upon college graduation was at Sears's corporate offices in Hoffman Estates, Illinois, where I worked as a merchandise analyst within the women's apparel buying offices. The commute from Chicago to Hoffman Estates would often take a brutal two hours, so soon after, I switched gears when offered a job with Franco Sarto footwear. My role for Franco Sarto included visiting countless retailers within the Midwestern region, ranging from independent retailers to big-box stores such as Dillards, Macy's, Lord & Taylor, and my retail alma mater, Nordstrom. Additionally, I worked closely with the marketing team to prepare for Franco Sarto personal appearances and other in-store, special events while also attending no less than six trade shows a year. At only 24 years of age, I was certain that I had my dream job for that time in my life. It turns out, though, that dreams can grow, and by 25, I was offered the chance to relocate to Franco Sarto's headquarters in Boston to become the company's national marketing director. I was beyond thrilled.

My excitement to take on more responsibility was off the charts, but a part of me was unsure about this cross-country move because of my father's recent diagnosis of brain cancer. Being both a proud father and a marketing pro himself, my dad encouraged me to go and not look back. With his approval, I packed my bags and was on my way.

Working with a wholesaler such as Franco Sarto gave me such incredible opportunities to learn more not only about the vendor side of the business but also about the retail side of the business. At the time, Franco Sarto was outperforming most of its competition, including Nine West, at retailers small and large; and as a result, my responsibilities were always evolving. Among them included trying to seek national press for Franco Sarto's growing brand.

Working with consumer publications that included *Lucky* and *Glamour* magazines as well as the trade publications *Footwear News*, *Women's Wear Daily*, and many others exposed me to a whole new side of retail. Instinctively, I loved the combination of retail and media, and it was at this time that I started to identify how I might be able to apply this duo in my own unique way to help independent retailers in the future.

Fast forward to a couple of years later, and I was ready to return to Chicago. Although I loved my job, I loved my father more. His cancer had advanced, and I knew that he would pass sooner than later, which made my decision to spend as much time as I could with him a priority. Although it was a tough choice to leave a job that I adored, I was fortunate that Bennett Footwear, the then-owner of Franco Sarto, offered to relocate me and give me a new position that could be based in the Midwest. Saying goodbye to my marketing days was extremely tough, but I embraced my new challenge as an account executive for Franco Sarto's sister footwear brand Etienne Aigner.

The following year introduced me to lots of change, most notably spending my days surrounded by numbers. Managing and selling inventory are no easy tasks, particularly when you are working with retailers that budget close to a million dollars or more just for your brand alone. Looking back, I refer to this point of my career as my own personal retail math boot camp. It was fast, furious, and unforgettable. I learned a lot, made some mistakes, and ultimately decided that being an account manager wasn't for me. I missed my marketing days, so I quietly looked around for a new opportunity that would allow me to do marketing again. Fortunately, Adidas was rolling out an in-store and major accounts marketing manager position based in Chicago, and I was lucky enough to get the job.

Working with Adidas, I was exposed to a whole new world of retailers that included Dick's Sporting Goods, Gander Mountain, and countless specialty retailers that served niche markets, including soccer, swim, and tennis. Moreover, this was the first time I worked for a company that was not only a retailer but also a wholesaler. Adidas has its own stores and also sells to other stores—which, as you can imagine, has both challenges and benefits. Once again, I considered myself fortunate to gain new experience and learn from some of the most well-respected retailers in the business. Meeting David Beckham and other Adidas athletes wasn't a bad job perk either.

Despite a great job and the chance to manage a team of over 30 people, I could feel a radical change brewing within me. I desperately wanted to control my time more after years of constant travel, and I also hoped to share everything I had learned with smaller, more mom-and-pop-style merchants. After only a couple of years with Adidas, I was finally ready to begin my own unique retail journey without an employer to officially report to. Like countless other entrepreneurs and possibly even like yourself, I decided to become my own boss. Friends and family thought for sure owning a little boutique of my own would be in my future, but instead I wanted to work with boutiques, retailers, and small-business owners—sharing with them what I could to help them in their unique goals. In 2007, Retail Minded was officially born.

Taglined a boutique consulting firm, Retail Minded aimed to support retailers within my immediate Chicago community. At this same time, I began writing a blog—a new trend that was emerging along with social media sites such as Twitter. Fairly quickly, my blog became recognized as a destination for independent retailers to gain news, education, and support for their businesses. This soon took over as my tagline, and I also began to accept freelance writing assignments for trade publications that included *Smart Retailer, Dance Retailer News, Museums & More, Crain's Chicago Business, Western Retailer,* and even Forbes.com. Without intentionally trying, my love for media and retail had grown into a functioning business, and soon after, my one-on-one consulting was pushed aside. I realized that through media, I could reach many more retailers with my goal of sharing independent specific news, education, and support; and it is through media that I did exactly that.

The years that followed introduced me to many new media clients as well as select consulting projects. It's also during this time that I first met my coauthor, Jason Prescott, founder and CEO of JP Communications, Inc., which represents companies that include TopTenWholesale.com and Manufacturer.com.

Despite a full schedule, I wanted to reach more retailers in a way that I believed they weren't being reached yet. There were and still are hundreds of publications committed to retail audiences, yet none focuses on the total lifestyle of being an independent retailer—whether selling shoes, hardware, home goods, or anything else. To me, this means supporting this unique audience of retailers with all the details of their businesses—not just those that fell within their store walls. In other words, I wanted discussions about insurance, health, family, time management, and more to be regular contributions to a publication that retailers could really relate to and one that was solely committed to independent retailers, not big-box merchants. It's with this in mind that *Retail Minded Magazine* came to life.

Without a formal publishing background or extensive media experience, I launched *Retail Minded Magazine* in January 2011. My quiet launch was well received by my already loyal blog followers, and with the help of my unique distribution model, the Retail Minded Partner Program, *Retail Minded Magazine* now reaches over 150,000 readers with each quarterly issue. This untraditional avenue of distribution allows niche retail groups such as Crafter's Home or the Museum Store Association, as well as local and state-level retail organizations such as the State Chamber of Oklahoma, the Florida Retail Federation, Minnesota Main Street, and others, to distribute *Retail Minded Magazine* as a membership benefit and educational resource to their members.

The same year I rolled out *Retail Minded Magazine*, I also introduced the independent retailer conference for the first time in July 2011 alongside my conference cofounder, Kerry Bannigan, of Nolcha Fashion Week: New York. Since then, this annual event has grown in both size and recognition, welcoming independent retailers and retail supporters to gain hands-on knowledge about trends specific in the independent retail scene. In March 2014, the Independent Retailer Conference was proudly introduced as our first pop-up conference at the nation's largest consumer trade show, the ASD Show, held biannually in Las Vegas.

The Retail Minded world has certainly grown since it's baby days back in 2007; yet, like much of my audience, we are still small and independent ourselves. I know firsthand the struggle to get a full day's work in and still feel like I haven't worked enough, as well as the constant juggling act to find time for family, friends, and—dare I say it—even myself. My team remains small, but our mission is always growing. I consider it both a privilege and a responsibility to support independent retailers, which is why I was so honored to join Jason Prescott in authoring this book to do just that.

It's my hope that you will take away from this book tips, tricks, and practical solutions to apply to your unique retail business. Whether you are a seasoned merchant or retail newbie, the content throughout this book is aimed at helping you to manage, market, and grow your retail business. Together Jason and I have uncovered resources, identified solutions, and compiled a collective spot for you to confidently refer to as you continue your retail journey. Also, we've interviewed over 50 industry leaders and retailers, allowing you to gain multiple perspectives on the dynamic world of retail. We've also provided you with Action Guides that follow each chapter, giving you next steps and how-to instructions to help your business succeed.

I'd like to believe that, like me, you look at your job as a privilege; and, therefore, that you are constantly seeking new ways to improve your business. Whether this is true or not, I hope that this book can deliver new ways for you to find success and achieve your unique retail goals. Thank you for giving us the opportunity to help you accomplish this—we hope you enjoy the ride.

PART I

Being Indie in a Big-Box World

1

Standing Out among Other Retailers

In order to be irreplaceable, one must always be different.

—*Coco Chanel (1883–1971), founder of Chanel, fashion designer*

To gain success in retail, merchants must create an environment and an experience that customers want to visit again and again. California-based retailer Kimberly Efseaff agrees with this, sharing her thoughts about where a customer's experience begins:

> The experience of a store should start before a customer even walks in the door. When someone sees your signage or peeks in the window, there should be a wow factor. It should captivate them and make them want to investigate your business, even if it's not something they may normally be drawn to. Once they do walk in, they should feel like

they are experiencing something that is totally unique and unlike any other store they have ever been to. The colors, products, atmosphere, design, aesthetics, and all other store details will help make this happen or, for that matter, not happen. Ultimately, a store should *feel* as unique as it *looks*. If you do this correctly, your customer will become captivated and engaged in your business.[1]

Engaging customers is key, and retailers such as Efseaff know that this is essential to creating, keeping, and growing business. The question is, however, just how do you do this? I've interviewed over 50 industry leaders who include retailers, wholesalers, trade show directors, magazine editors, retail organization leaders, and more to help answer this question. All of them share their unique expertise and perspectives on how you can find store success in the competitive world of retail. With a heavy emphasis on independent brick-and-mortar retailers, this book will look at the many layers involved in managing and marketing a retail store today. From there, it will help introduce you to new ideas, reshape old habits, and identify the trends of retail designed to keep modern merchants visible and successful. Among the main goals of this book will also be to introduce retailers to external players, ranging from business resources to trade shows to retail associations and more.

Illinois-based retailer Angela Gianfrancesco, whose store, Stella Blue Design, resides just a mile west of Chicago's Wrigley Field, considers learning from outside influencers a key strategy in helping her own business grow. "I may only have one store and be the sole store owner, but I never feel alone in running it. Through RetailMinded.com, my local Chamber of Commerce, a great staff, and merchant friends, I constantly feel like I am learning new things and have people to turn to when I have questions."

As an independent retailer, it's easy to forget that you have so many advocates on your side to help your business thrive. One of the main goals of this book is to help retailers regain their trust and support from outside players, welcoming a variety of businesses and people into their niche worlds to help them further succeed in retail. In the chapters that follow, we'll unveil organizations, associations, and retail-specific groups that have your best interest in mind, as well as identify why your participation with them matters. We will also discuss the value in working with your local community to increase your store and town's independent retail awareness. We will also provide details on how you can become more involved in the increasingly popular buy-local movements. Most important, however, we will identify practical ways for you to keep your doors open in a competitive retail environment, sharing expert yet realistic insight on how you can do this. As retailer Gianfrancesco stresses, "I have been open since 2010, and since then, I can count on my hand how many days I have gone to work without learning something new about customer care or store management. Zero. Every day, every customer, and every situation teaches me something that can improve my business."

It's with this in mind that the chapters that follow were created. Every chapter, every detail, and every resource identified is intended to help you with your business. As an independent merchant, however, it's up to you to decide just how you will apply these details to your own unique store. To further support you, each chapter concludes with an Action Guide intended to help you take immediate steps in helping your business. Collectively, we hope that these Action Guides push you to look at your store or future store via a new perspective while also encouraging you to do things you may never have done before.

Finally, remember to stay enthusiastic, optimistic, and accepting of challenges as they come your way—because they will—as you embark on your retail journey. Whether you're a veteran merchant or a new store owner, retail as we know it is changing at a pace faster than ever before. As a result, you should be ready for both ups and downs along the way. This book will help you to understand the latest trends, expected growth, and anticipated opportunities specific to independent retailers, and we hope that you enjoy the experience of the chapters ahead.

Action Guide

Embracing change isn't always an easy task, particularly for entrepreneurs who choose to follow their own individual paths. Change, however, is a critical component of keeping up with customers, inventory, and sales.

To help you to identify your comfort for change, answer the following questions with either yes or no:

1. Have you introduced a new vendor into your store assortment in the last three months?
2. Have you eliminated a vendor from your store assortment within the last six months?
3. Do you actively seek outside, external resources to help you learn more about managing your business, possi-

bly including a consultation, education course, or other learning scenario?

4. Have you identified your target customer?

5. Do you believe that your target customer is your actual customer?

6. Do you want to gain a new generation of customers in your store, such as Generation Y?

7. Do you actively solicit publicity for your store, either from an outside public relations support or from your own internal efforts?

8. Do you have a solid online presence, allowing you to gain recognition in online searches on websites such as Google or Yahoo?

9. Are you a member of no less than one retail-specific group?

10. Do you have employees who are either part or full time but not seasonal?

For every yes you answered, give yourself 10 points. Based on a traditional grading scale of 0 to 100, total your points to identify your grade as a current retailer. Are you at 50 points? If so, that gives you an F in your retail performance, playing you at 50 percent in score. Are you at 70 percent? That's a C, which represents an average performance, yet it is just one point away from below average. If you scored at 80 percent or above, well done! You are doing a great job at retail; however, like all things in life, there's always room to improve. Whether you failed or thrived in this basic retail evaluation, we look forward to helping you achieve stronger retail success by offering you expert insight, additional action guides, and much more in the chapters ahead.

2

Stepping Outside
Your Comfort Zone

I am always doing that which I cannot do,
in order that I may learn how to do it.

—*Pablo Picasso (1881–1973), painter and artist*

A CCORDING TO Joe Abraham, author of *Entrepreneurial DNA*, there are four kinds of entrepreneurs. Builder, opportunist, specialist, and innovator represent the various personalities of owners of small, medium-sized, and large businesses when it comes to being their own boss. Although independent retailers will embody one or more of these four entrepreneurial DNA personalities, all entrepreneurial personalities are likely to create the habit of working within their own comfort zone.

Having founded our own businesses, we can relate firsthand to the challenges of being an entrepreneur. We can also speak to the habits that shape our daily actions, many of which keep us acutely focused and working comfortably within familiar territory, both literally and figuratively. More important, however, we've also experienced firsthand the benefits of stepping outside our comfort zone. As a result, we push ourselves to do this more often than not. Our experiences aside, what really matters here is consumers' reactions to *your* habits.

Whether you consider yourself an old-fashioned retailer, a modern merchant, or an up-and-coming store owner, a critical component to your retail success is identifying your strengths, weaknesses, and potential to do better. With over half of small-business owners closing their doors within two years of opening them, it's imperative to consider all available opportunities to succeed. This is particularly crucial considering the nature of today's competitive marketplace. Consumers have a tremendous number of choices when it comes to making their buying decisions, and independent retailers should attempt to stand out versus blend in when it comes to staying competitive.

New York–based merchant Macquenzi Farquer, who owns gift and specialty store Lockport in the Astoria neighborhood of New York City, suggests that independent retailers need to identify direct competition at the very beginning and understand how they can compete with it from a realistic perspective:

Big-box stores can deliver real headaches for independent merchants. There is nothing worse for a small-business owner to hear that the same product they carry is being sold for less at a big-box store. I recognize that this price comparison will happen; however, I also recognize that most consumers will not understand the rhyme or reason why. This said, I try to challenge myself to provide the best inventory assortment I can to better compete with big-box stores. Inevitably, my inventory will be compared to that of other retailers, and I try to buy more unique inventory to deal with this.[1]

Challenging yourself to offer a variety of merchandise can certainly help to attract consumers and increase purchases. However, identifying the right assortment of inventory is often the challenge that retailers face. For Farquer, this meant identifying what her local customers wanted and then identifying the appropriate blend of price and product to offer her consumers. In doing this, she stepped outside her comfort zone to create an edge against her local retail competition:

> For my customers, finding stock furniture for their typically smaller, urban living spaces is a challenge. For me, it's also a challenge to stock furniture in my limited square foot store. While my customer is constantly asking for this, I have learned that no matter what I can offer, I can't compete against my two closest big-box competitors, IKEA or CB2. Instead, I call my furniture selection "finishing pieces" and market them as the special detail you layer with more affordable pieces from national chains.[2]

Tackling the job of understanding the local consumers' behaviors helped Farquer to identify a smart strategic plan to stay relevant

RETAIL TIP

Do not ignore that many—if not all—of your customers include big-box stores, national chains, or discount centers as regular destinations to shop. Instead, identify the best ways to support these customers knowing that they are also shopping at your competitors. Among the ways in which you can do this include introducing diverse inventory, providing stronger customer care, hosting in-store events, supporting community events, and being a familiar, friendly face within your own store.

Brick and mortar retailer Cynthia Sutton is a retail veteran, having previously worked in the buying offices for major retailer Claire's Boutique prior to opening her own store, The Silver Barn, in Columbus, Texas, in 2008. Selling everything from home décor to baby gifts, Sutton recognizes that big-box stores are her competition and believes there is room for all types of retailers.

"Big-box stores and independent retailers *can* compliment each other. The key is for independent retailers to offer unique items that are not easily found in department stores or other big-box merchants. It's our job to search for specialty items and vendors not found in these stores, offering something unique to our customers."

Whether your store stocks everyday basics or specialty items, it's important to recognize how you stack up against big-box competition. Make it a priority to know what they're selling so you can decide what best suits your store shelves and customers, as well. Take the time to visit your competitor's stores on no less than a quarterly basis, recognizing anything new they have done to their stores. This may include the introduction of new vendors, bold display changes, customer service enhancements, or anything else that stands out.

While visiting your competition may not seem like a valuable addition to our to-do-list, it's possible that it's among the most valuable things you can do as a business owner. Always know what your competition is up to in an effort to stay competitive against them.

in her Astoria, New York, neighborhood. Her solution of providing "finishing details" versus traditional stock furniture has differentiated her from big-box retailers while also opening up a niche sales strategy. This approach also places her outside a traditional retail comfort zone by acknowledging and actually discussing the use of big-box inventory in combination with her own.

Inventory is a critical component of any store's success, yet well beyond what fills your store shelves is how you market, manage, and sell it. These actions can make or break a retailer's livelihood, yet many retailers fall into habits that work against their sales goals.

Gevena, Illinois–based retailer Shari Ralish, whose store Peaceful Parlour provides herbal teas, earth-friendly products, artisan work, and more, is an example of an independent merchant who fell victim to being set in her old ways:

When I opened my store in February 2010, I merchandised it and stocked it with products I thought customers wanted because I wanted them as well. It took me a few years to truly understand my local consumers, and even then my floor plan didn't accommodate their shopping patterns or my total store assortment. It wasn't until 2012 that I finally let an outside retail specialist come in and help me see my store through another person's eyes. The changes in inventory, store layout, and my overall marketing initiatives have helped to increase my sales by over 37 percent in the past year alone."[3]

Forcing yourself to let others affect how you operate your store can be a difficult challenge for some, particularly if you have an entrepreneurial personality that prefers independence and control. Yet identifying this as a weakness in your entrepreneurial DNA can actually help you in your success as a merchant.

Joe Abraham, author of *Entrepreneurial DNA*, believes that most retailers "will run into some common challenges when operating their stores. Knowing upfront what their operational weaknesses and strengths are can actually empower them to align with advisors, partners, and service providers who complement their weaknesses. Without addressing their own entrepreneurial characteristics, retailers risk a frustrating journey or worse, the demise of their businesses."[4]

Habits of Successful Retailers

While closing your doors is certainly not the goal, identifying the top habits of effective retailers should be. Here in no particular order are 10 habits of highly effective retailers. In the chapters that follow, we will explore each of these in detail.

14

Habit 1: Know Who Your Customers Are

Often retailers open their stores with a visual image of their typical consumer that may not be accurate. Using modern data, including point-of-sale (POS) and other tracking systems, to help identify who your actual customers are, you can help to identify who is truly spending money at your store. In this regard, there's no such thing as too much information.

Habit 2: Understand How Your Customers Shop

Knowing who your customers are is one thing, but understanding how they shop is an entirely different thing. Seek consumer insight by asking questions via social media, through in-store conversations, by offering quick surveys via e-mail or your website, and using other data-collecting methods that address the needs, wants, and actions of your customers. Good old-fashioned observation goes a long way here as well. Be organized by aggregating and categorizing your research.

Habit 3: React to the Information You Gain from Customers

The worst thing you could do is gain quality insight into your customers and then fail to act on it. Make it a priority to constantly evaluate your customers. Listen to what they are asking for, identify what they are not interested in with your product assortment or shopping experience, and try to capture their wishes as a consumer. Acknowledging both their wants and lack of interest is a great way to discover what and how you should be selling.

Habit 4: Be Where Your Competition Is

While you may never have a thousand stores like your nearest big-box neighbor, you can be where they are when it comes to your marketing efforts. Do not neglect social media or your local market media. Seek coverage in your area publications, participate in local events, and be visible beyond your store walls, including online.

Habit 5: Compare Yourself with Others

Remember when your mother used to tell you not to compare yourself with your peers? Well, we're throwing that advice out the window. In the case of retail, you want to always compare yourself with your nearby merchants. This will identify not only the ways you are different but also the ways you are alike. Learning from others' mistakes is much less painful—and often less costly—than learning from your own.

Habit 6: Train Your Employees *and* Yourself

No matter what you may think, you simply don't know it all. No one does. Challenge yourself to constantly learn something new about your business. Whether it is store operations or a new vendor, there's always something to research. Additionally, make sure that your team learns new updates on store procedures, products, industry trends, social media features, and more. All employees, even part-time or seasonal employees, can gain from scheduled training sessions that help to position them not only to learn more but also to feel as if they are key players in the success of your business.

Habit 7: Support Other Local Businesses

Nobody likes the person who doesn't practice what they preach. For independent retailers, this holds especially true. Support your fellow local merchants as much as possible. The old saying, "What goes around comes around," holds very true here and should not be taken lightly. Instead, embrace other local businesses not only by shopping at them but also by referring them.

Habit 8: Attend Trade Shows Regularly

Most trade shows nowadays offer more than just the opportunity to buy inventory. Many, such as the ASD Trade Show, held biannually in Las Vegas, provide educational experiences, networking events, social opportunities, and more. Take advantage of all that trade shows have to offer, including the chance to connect face to face with your existing vendors and discover new vendors as well.

Habit 9: Seek New Ways to Manage Your Business

Our modern world is constantly introducing new technologies and other ways to help businesses of all kinds thrive. For retailers, it's especially important to evaluate service providers and available technology that can help you operate your store more efficiently. Neglecting commercial evolution can cause you to drift apart from your retail peers and, ultimately, from your consumers.

Habit 10: Be Open to Part-Time or Full-Time Employees

It's easy to fall into the habit of working every day in your store without ever taking a break. However, working in your store full time does not allow you to accomplish many of the other suggested habits on this list and also limits you from simply getting a break. Successful retailers, even those with only one store, are often more successful because they budget for part-time or full-time employees. As a result, their performance as a store owner is not compromised, and instead, they reap the rewards of a more balanced work schedule and stronger sales.

Humans are creatures of comfort, and retailers are no exception. It can get really cozy settling into your ways, but push yourself to step outside your comfort zone to really allow yourself and your store to evolve and thrive.

* * *

In the chapters that follow, we'll identify how to incorporate retail best practices into your business; share preferred resources for independent retailers; introduce contact details for various retail associations; explain how to solicit and manage your own press; offer ways to market your store both online and offline; and explain why incorporating a buy-local campaign would be good for sales. In addition, we'll offer you expert insight into managing your inventory, social media, employees, and, of course, customers.

Action Guide

When trying to understand your own strengths and weaknesses as a retailer, it's important to recognize your operational habits as a merchant. Answer the following questions, and record your responses, allowing you to reference your habits in the chapters ahead and, ultimately, reflect on the necessary changes you may need to make to enhance your business.

1. What operational procedures does your store routinely perform today that it did not one year ago?
2. If you have been open longer than three years, what three additional store operations are conducted that you were not doing 36 months ago?
3. Have your core inventory categories changed since you first opened your store? Why or why not?
4. Do your most popular items sell based on circumstance, such as a customer finding a unique gift he or she loves,

or is it more strategic, such as replenishing a household item that customers know you have in stock?

5. Do you provide employee training for store operations, new products, or any other reason? If so, how often do you do this?

6. What customer-service expectations does your store have in place? How is this measured among your employees and yourself?

7. What marketing strategies do you consistently lean on to promote your store to both existing and new customers?

8. How often do you seek attention from the media with a formal press release or organized media pitch?

9. What day-to-day habits do you identify as mandatory in your store, such as stock replenishment, merchandising, or cold calling customers?

10. What is on your wish list for the years ahead as your store continues to grow?

Take the time to honestly answer these questions, pushing yourself to be truthful with your responses. Often simply acknowledging your routine habits in comparison with suggested other ones can help you in stepping outside your comfort zone. In the chapters that follow, we'll dive into the details of how this can be accomplished.

3

Leaning on Outside Organizations

If you do what you've always done,
you'll get what you've always gotten.

—*Tony Robbins (1960–present), life coach,*
author, motivational speaker

"THE NUMBER one job of a business owner is to run a great business, so it would be short-sighted not to take full advantage of opportunities provided to help businesses achieve greater success," Office of Main Street New Jersey and Improvement District Programs of New Jersey's Jef Buehler states. While we could not agree more, it's often easier said than done when it comes to supporting your business with the many resources available to you. Often business owners get lost in their everyday hustle and bustle without ever seeking outside support to make their jobs easier. Luckily, there is a vast and diverse group of both private- and public-sector organizations that can help you achieve stronger retail success.

Retailers should look at their local communities, state-level organizations, and national groups in an effort to identify support that makes sense for them and their unique businesses. Beginning at a local level, most retailers have access to municipal support, including city meetings, education resources, and local Chamber of Commerce support. Although each community has its own varied operational resources that benefit retailers specifically, all retailers have support beyond their local towns. State-level organizations, such as the Retail Association of Maine and the Kentucky Retail Federation, provide tremendous support for retailers of all sizes.

Getting Involved with Outside Organizations

Getting engaged at your local level is absolutely vital in building toward your business success, particularly if selling online or beyond your local area is not part of your business plan. This local-level participation will give you support and insight into your customers, competition, and community that state-level and national organizations often cannot.

Ellen Divita, economic development director for the City of Geneva, Illinois, explains just how valuable local cities and Chambers of Commerce can be to a small-business owner:

Your local city and chamber offer a variety of resources to retailers, including visibility and credential to your business. Because trust is such an important component in the marketplace these days, this is especially important to consider as a business owner of any kind. Local city and chamber offices offer many resources, including assistance with the development and opening process, permits, and licenses. The nontangible assistance can prove even more valuable, which includes building relationships locally that can deliver the visibility and credential that your business needs.[1]

Furthermore, Divita stresses the importance of respecting consumer options:

People have choices when it comes to where they shop, and consumers will buy from retailers they trust. Being referred and trusted by the chamber and your local city government is like being prescreened, which is critical for retailers considering the immense amount of competition they have. Unlike national retailers, whose return policies and other customer expectations are more known, independent retailers need to gain the trust of their consumers. Your local chamber and city can help you achieve a strong reputation that gives customers the trust they are looking for.[2]

Being known in your community for what you offer can be priceless when cross-referrals happen organically as the result of satisfied customers, community participation, and your commitment to delivering a strong in-store and city experience. Furthermore, many local Chambers of Commerce and city organizations provide educational resources, local media support, and other community-based incentives that can help merchants gain stronger customer awareness. Beyond your local organizations, however, it's important to look at state-level retail associations that can help your business from a broader perspective as well.

EXPERT SPOTLIGHT

Harriet Parker, manager of the Illinois Small Business Development Center at Waubonsee Community College in Aurora, Illinois, suggests that working with outside organizations can help retailers and other small business owners gain access to expert support that is often free or at a reduced rate. Also, Parker shares her insight on how ongoing support versus only when needed can help retailers.

"By working with organizations such as Small Business Development Centers (SBDCs), retailers are able to access expertise they may be lacking, as well as resources they may not know about. Our organizations, like many others, often have business experts ready to help retailers go beyond their own capabilities to build stronger businesses. In addition, we encourage retailers not to wait until they are experiencing a problem to seek assistance, but instead treat these resources as an ongoing partner for their business team. Whether it is for a problem, a brainstorming session, or nearly anything else, SBDC's and other support organizations should be viewed as trusted advisors to help retailers."

To get started in seeking outside support from your local SBDC, Parker suggests visiting www.sba.gov and clicking on the Get Local Assistance link. From there, making a phone call to their offices is typically all it takes to get started.[3]

Andy Ellen, president and general counsel of the North Carolina Retail Merchants Association, explains that associations like his are intended to act as part of a retailer's own team:

> We see ourselves as an extension of a retailer's staff. Our reason for being is to promote and advocate for the retail industry, so we make it a priority to be experts on all issues that will impact a retailer's store operations as well as develop strong relationships with policy makers in our state. If you have a problem or an issue, it is quite likely that your state retail association has already encountered this issue for another retailer and has the answer to your question at their fingertips.[4]

In addition, Ellen believes that retail organizations such as the North Carolina Retail Merchants Association help deliver solutions to common and uncommon retail challenges:

> State retail associations are problem solvers. We understand state governments and know how to cut through the red tape and voice mail jungle of state and local governments to assist retailers. Collectively, state-level associations promote the retail industry through the press, often highlighting a local retailer's great practices or success. This translates to free PR and advertising for retailers, provided by a trusted source—us.[5]

In addition to bringing media attention and helping to solve retail challenges, state-level retail associations support merchants in their everyday operations. Additional support that associations often offer includes discounts on store services that retailers need, such as credit card processing, and expert insight into state-specific laws and other regulatory agencies such as the departments of revenue, transportation, or labor.

Curtis Picard, executive director of the Retail Association of Maine, describes the benefits of working with state-level associations as "insurance for retailers":

> When retailers become members of their state-level associations, they gain full-time representation for legislative issues, networking with other like-minded retailers, and access to a number of money-saving programs that can help their business save money directly and operate more efficiently. We like to think of ourselves as insurance for retailers. We help protect you for a very low cost.[6]

Although legislative support may not be on the top of your list of ways to be supported, it certainly should be explored. State and national legislative decisions affect merchants in a variety of ways, and too often retailers don't know how they will affect them until it's too late. Picard explains:

> When you don't communicate with your state-level retail association, it means that your voice does not get heard. I can't tell you how often I hear from nonmember retailers when they call after something bad was passed by the legislature. First, they had no idea that certain legislation was being considered, and second, they had no opportunity to share how it would impact them.[7]

In addition to getting active in your state-level associations, Picard believes that local and trade-specific groups are also imperative to your retail success:

> I have always told potential members that they need to belong to three associations. First, you need to belong to your local Chamber of Commerce or downtown business association. That is where your business is and where your employees live and work. Moreover, you should belong to your specific industry trade association, such as the Craft and Hobby Association for craft-based retailers. And last, you should belong to a statewide association because most legislation happens at the state level, and you need eyes and ears looking out for your business. In most cases, a state retail association will fill that role.[8]

Trade-specific organizations are typically nationally based, although many offer regional groups as well. Nearly every sector of retail, from flowers to footwear to handbags to home decor, has retail-specific trade groups that help to support merchants selling their specific product category. Among their top roles in supporting retailers is delivering education through annual events, publications, webinars, and other avenues.

Jama Rice, executive director and CEO of the Museum Store Association, explains that niche groups such as hers offer "opportunities and resources for like-minded members and other stakeholders to share best practices; look to the association's industry standards to achieve professional excellence; rely on benchmarking statistics for performance analysis; access publications and online communities and attend face-to-face meetings and conferences for technical and educational content specific to nonprofit retailing; and connect with affiliated vendors for sourcing unique products."[9]

With such an extensive range of benefits to gain from, it seems foolish not to get involved in organizations such as your local Chamber of Commerce, city or state retail association, or niche retail groups. Missy Brozek, vice president and creative director of craft and hobby retail group Crafters' Home, agrees that this is extremely important for merchants, particularly as retail becomes even more competitive:

> As retail gets more and more competitive, I'm convinced that independent stores will need to keep banding together to thrive. The benefits are just too good to ignore. Building a group gives retailers opportunities to collaborate and learn from one another without feeling like they're supporting their direct competitors. In the case of niche retail groups, it also opens up the opportunity to lean on one another for more specific support, reducing the need to reinvent the wheel for promotions, marketing, and events. At Crafters' Home, we put together fully worked-out programs to share with our group based on our experience and the experience of our members. Maybe most important, however, there's strength in numbers. It's so important that we make sure that manufacturers hear, respond to, and respect the collective voice of independent retailers.[10]

Benefits That Organizations May Offer

As a merchant, it's possible that you fall into more than one specific retail sector. Therefore, you may be a potential candidate to belong to more than one retail-specific group. You will want to consider how participating in multiple groups will help your business, particularly because they typically have a membership fee applied to them. Whether you are in one group or more, however, you should evaluate what benefits you gain by participating in each. Among the variety of benefits that retail groups as well as state-level retail associations may offer are the following:

- *Conferences and trade shows.* Retail-specific groups typically host annual, biannual, and/or regional events to support their participating retailers. Sometimes these events are open to anyone, but members gain a discount when attending or can attend as part of their annual dues. Either way, these events are designed to deliver key support in a niche retail market, providing you with expert education, access to vendors, face-to-face networking opportunities, and more.
- *Buyers' guides.* A buyer's guide uniquely created for your retail sector is a valuable resource, particularly considering how busy retailers are. Retail trade organizations often create annual buyers' guides that give you quick, convenient, and trusted access to industry-specific products and services. Retail Minded also provides an annual "Resource Guide" that focuses on store operations and preferred resources for running your business, such as online marketing and e-mail management, which is available at RetailMinded.com.

- *Private online groups.* Being active in a membership-based group will introduce you to other retailers similar to you. This opens up a fantastic opportunity to learn from others, lean on others, and leverage what other retailers have done in their own retail efforts. Online chat groups, private discussion boards, and membership-controlled groups can provide you with the chance to gain insight and expertise from other like-minded retailers. Some state-level retail associations offer this, and most retail niche groups provide this as a membership perk as well.

- *Health and business insurance programs.* The buying power of an association versus your individual buying power can save you money when it comes to buying insurance. Leveraging the discounts or preferred rates available to state retail associations or retail-specific groups not only can help you save money but also can provide you with stronger insurance coverage. Be sure to cross-reference updated insurance options no less than annually because often these will change and your options may be affected as well.

- *Market research and trend information.* In the same manner that state-level organizations may provide up-to-date news on taxes and other legislative issues, national retail-specific groups will share the latest on industry trends, market research, and niche information for your retail sector. Applying up-to-date industry news and information to your business can only aid you in your overall retail success and thus should always be on your to-do list.

- *Merchant solution benefits.* Whether your store is solely online, a brick-and-mortar establishment, or both, processing payments is a critical part of your operational plan. Retail groups can help you achieve better rates in your payment-processing solutions while also supporting you in your payment software solutions. Many of these benefits also include top-notch customer service that is provided as a membership advantage, offering an invaluable resource when you face payment-processing challenges.

- *Industry publications.* Gaining retail-rich content is no easy task, but most retail-specific groups work hard to deliver quality information to their members. Most of these groups seek expert insight on a variety of retail subjects to share with their members, and many are part of Retail Minded's "Partner Program"—sharing additional news, education, and support from Retail Minded through a quarterly magazine and other retail news publications. Using the magazines, newsletters, e-blasts, and blogs that these organizations provide can help you achieve more knowledge for your business. The key, of course, is to combine this knowledge with information about annual events, trade shows, vendors, and all other information you can gain to achieve the greatest success in your store operations and sales.

- *Travel discounts.* Travel is likely part of your annual schedule, particularly if you are active in trade shows and educational events. Many retail groups recognize this and provide discounted rates for airfare, car rentals, and hotels. Taking advantage of these discounts can help save you some hard-earned dollars.

Although many retail group benefits exceed those just listed, the only way they work is if you get involved. Below are some examples of such retail groups, although we encourage you to look beyond these associations for ones that make sense for your retail business.

American Apparel & Footwear Association
WeWear.org
ART Home Furnishings Network
AccessoriesResourceTeam.org
Craft and Hobby Retailers
Craft & Hobby Association, www.craftandhobby.org
Floral Retailers
Society of American Florists, www.safnow.org
Home Furnishings Industry
Accessories Resource Team (ART), www.accessoriesresource-
    team.org
Independent Jewelry Retailers and Vendors
Retail Jewelers Organization, www.rjomemebers.com
Independent Pet Retailers
NexPet, www.nexpet.com
Museum and Not-for-Profit Stores
Museum Store Association, www.museumstoreassociation.org
Specialty Toy Industry
American Specialty Toy Retailing Association (ASTRA),
    www.astratoy.org

In addition to the various retail groups that exist, it's important to seek additional support for your store if you feel that there is a void not being filled. This may mean reaching out to retail consultants, participating in retail education events such as Retail Minded's annual independent retailer conference, calling your local SCORE or small-business development center, and leaning on mentors you have identified who can uniquely help *you*. Remember, it often takes stepping outside your comfort zone to reach your retail potential. These groups and businesses exist with this in mind and want to help you in achieving your best retail success yet.

* * *

In Chapter 4, we'll discuss the value of shaping your store to be uniquely yours. Also, we'll discuss how inventory plays a critical role in shaping your store's reputation and personality, as well as identify various characteristics of a store that help to make it unique. Finally, we'll offer you suggested interview questions for hiring potential employees and share additional details to help make your store one of a kind.

Action Guide

Your local Chambers of Commerce, main street programs, city contacts, and business groups can help you achieve stronger business engagement with your community. Using the Web as well as local resources such as your area library, identify who to contact, and make it a priority to get involved right away.

Beyond local support, use the following list to obtain contact details for your state retail association. A number of states, including Oklahoma, Wisconsin, and Alaska, are not part of the Council of State Retail Associations. Some states, however, have statewide Chamber of Commerce associations instead. An example of this is the State Chamber of Oklahoma, which you can learn more about at www.okstatechamber.com.

For a complete list and more information about state-level retail associations, visit the Council of State Retail Association's website at www.councilsra.com.

Identify your state's contact information in the following list, and visit its website. Follow up directly via the contact information provided on the website or by using the phone number in the list to identify how becoming a member can help you in your retail goals.

State Retail Association	Business Phone	Website
Alabama Retail Association	(334) 263-5757	www.alabamaretail.org
Arizona Retailers Association	(480) 833-0009	www.azretailers.com
Arkansas Grocers and Retail Merchants Association	(501) 664-8680	www.agrma.org
Associated Oregon Industries Retail Council	(503) 588-0050	www.aoi.org
California Retailers Association	(916) 443-1975	www.calretailers.com
Colorado Retail Council	(303) 355-1066	www.coloradoretail.org
Connecticut Retail Merchants Association	(860) 527-1044	www.crmaonline.com

Delaware Retail Council, Inc.	(302) 576-6560	www.dscc.com /state_chamber
Florida Retail Federation	(850) 222-4082	www.frf.org
Georgia Retail Association	(678) 401-6061	www.georgiaretail.org
Idaho Retailers Association	(208) 342-0010	www.idahoretailers.org
Illinois Retail Merchants Association	(312) 726-4600	www.irma.org
Indiana Retail Council	(317) 632-7391	www.indianaretailers .com
Iowa Retail Federation	(515) 270-1729	www.iaretail.org
Kansas Chamber of Commerce	(785) 357-6321	www.kansaschamber .org
Kentucky Retail Federation	(502) 875-1444	www.kyretail.com
Louisiana Retailers Association	(225) 344-9481	www.laretail.org
Maryland Retailers Association	(410) 269-1440	www.mdra.org
Michigan Retailers Association	(517) 372-5656	www.retailers.com
Minnesota Retailers Association	(651) 227-6631	www.mnretail.org
Mississippi Retail and Grocers Association	(601) 362-8900	www.msrga.com
Missouri Retailers Association	(573) 636-5128	www.moretailers.com
Montana Retail Association	(406) 256-1005	www.mtretail.com
Nebraska Retail Federation	(402) 474-5255	www.nebraskaretail.com

New Jersey Retail Merchants Association	(609) 393-8006	www.njrma.org
New Mexico Retail Association	(505) 889-8906	www.nmretail association.com
North Carolina Retail Merchants Association	(919) 832-0811	www.ncrma.org
North Dakota Retail Association	(701) 223-3370	www.ndretail.org
Ohio Council of Retail Merchants	(614) 221-7833	www.ocrm.net
Pennsylvania Retailers' Association	(717) 233-7976	www.paretailers.org
Retail Association of Maine	(207) 623-1149	www.retailmaine.org
Retail Association of Nevada	(775) 882-1700	www.rannv.org
Retail Council of New York State	(518) 465-3586	www.retailcouncilnys .com
Retail Merchants Association of New Hampshire	(603) 225-9748	www.rmanh.com
Retail Merchants of Hawaii	(808) 592-4200	www.rmhawaii.org
Retailers Association of Massachusetts	(617) 523-1900	www.retailersma.org
Rhode Island Retail Federation	(401) 621-6106	www.provchamber.com
South Carolina Retail Association	(919) 832-0811	www.ncrma.org/scra
South Dakota Retailers Association	(605) 224-5050	www.sdra.org

Tennessee Retail Association	(615) 256-4771	www.tnretail.com
Texas Retailers Association	(512) 472-8261	www.txretailers.org
Utah Retail Merchants Association	(801) 262-5001	www.utahretail.com
Vermont Retail Association	(802) 839-1931	www.vtretailers.com
Virginia Retail Merchants Association	(804) 649-0789	www.virginiaretail.org
Washington Retail Association	(360) 943-9198	www.retailassociation .org
West Virginia Retailers Association	(304) 342-1183	www.wvretailers.com
Wyoming Retail Association	(307) 634-7768	www.wyoretail.org

4

Identifying Your Unique Store Story

The only way to do great work is to love what you do.

—Steve Jobs (1955–2011), entrepreneur, cofounder of Apple, Inc.

THE BEAUTIFUL thing about working with retail groups is that you gain strength in numbers, avoiding the sense of isolation that can weigh on an independent retailer. Although a support system and the power of a community are integral, you should also optimize the power of your unique merchant story.

Every retailer has his or her own story to tell. From how it came to life to why it retains customers, your store has a unique narrative whether you recognize it or not. Understanding this narrative can help you to stand out in the marketplace, allow you to better support your customers, and identify ways to keep your sales flowing.

To help you clearly identify your merchant story, consider why you became a retailer in the first place. Did you open a store because you love a certain category of product? Are you keeping your family business alive? Do you prefer to work for yourself versus others? Possibly, you became a retailer by accident as a result of doing something else. Whatever your reason for becoming a retailer, consider how it led you to where you are today. Then—even more important—consider whether your story is worth sharing. After all, if even *you* don't think it is, then why would a customer want to experience it?

* * *

Independent retailers are often considered local celebrities simply because of the fact that they have their own stores. Walking into your local grocer may mean seeing 10 familiar faces because they are customers of your business. Going to a local sporting event could translate to meeting potential new clients or seeing past customers you haven't seen in a long time. Essentially, as a retailer, you are never truly "off" and always working to improve and expand your identity. This type of commitment to your job is honorable and yet exhausting. Fortunately, even your own unique retail story comes with supporting characters. And as with any engaging narrative, every character has a message to share.

Creating an Inventory Assortment That Stands Out

Among your most popular supporting characters are the various brands that make up your store inventory and merchandising assortment. And just like any good story, characters will come and go. For a retailer, this may mean fading out of a particular category of inventory altogether or letting go of a vendor that is not performing well. The most boring story lines are those that never shuffle their characters, and for retailers, this means allowing inventory to become stale and uninviting.

"My biggest fear as a small brick-and-mortar store is that customers will not find my inventory exciting enough to want to buy," Chicago-based retailer Angela Gianfrancesco states. "For me, this means constantly seeking customer feedback, attending trade shows, evaluating what is selling and what's not, and introducing new products into my rotation to keep things fresh,"[1] Gianfrancesco continues.

Identifying a strong inventory assortment is critical when it comes to making a lasting impression on consumers, not to mention standing out among your local competition. Even the most beautiful retail stores are doomed to fail if their inventory assortment does not allure customers to buy. Finding the right combination of vendors and overall inventory can be a tough challenge, however.

"I don't think my store would still be open if I had not made attending shows a priority. Every show introduces me to new vendors while also giving me the chance to get face time with my existing vendors,"[2] Gianfrancesco explains.

Attending trade shows is a fantastic opportunity for merchants of all kinds. Whether you sell high-end, middle-tier, or dollar-priced items, there are trade shows that cater to you.

"Making it a priority to attend trade shows has never been my challenge, though I hear it can be a struggle for other retailers. My challenge is deciding which shows to attend and what vendors to buy from,"[3] states Gianfrancesco.

Identifying the best shows and the best vendors for your store is no easy task. You should consider shows that introduce you to relevant vendors from your niche retail sector, as well as larger shows that can introduce you to more diverse vendors and products. Typically, it's a good idea to attend no less than one retail-specific trade show and one general-merchandise trade show per year. For example, the Fashion Footwear Association of New York (FFANY) hosts a quarterly footwear show for footwear retailers. Merchants who primarily sell footwear would benefit from attending this show but would also benefit from attending a show such as the ASD Show in Las Vegas, a biannual show that offers a diverse assortment of general consumer merchandise. By participating in two distinctly different shows, you open up the opportunity for more range in your inventory assortment, stronger variety than your competition, and greater opportunities to identify impulse, seasonal, and must-have purchases for your store.

The following guide shares information on a variety of top trade shows held in the United States annually, as well as details on their target industries, show locations, dates, and websites. Although this list does not identify all available trade shows to retailers, it introduces you to some of the top shows in select retail markets.

TRADE SHOW GUIDE

Show Name	Industry	When	Where	
ASD	General Merchandise	February or March and August	Las Vegas, NV	a.
CES	Consumer Electronics	January	Las Vegas, NV	cesweb.org
Children's Club	Children's Clothing	January, March, August October	NYC, NY	enkshows.com /childrensclub
Couture	Couture Jewelry	February and May or June	NYC, NY Las Vegas, NV	national jeweler.com/cj/
ISS	Decorated Apparel		Various Locations	issshow.com
JCK	Jewelry	May, June, July, August, October	Las Vegas, NV; Toronto, Canada; Panama City	jckonline.com
MAGIC	Apparel and Accessories	February and August	Las Vegas, NV	magiconline .com
National Hardware Show	Hardware and Tools	May	Las Vegas, NV	nationalhard wareshow.com
New York International Gift Fair	Middle to High-End Gifts	January and August	NYC, NY	nyigf.com
PGA Show	Golf Industry	January	Orlando, FL	pgashow.com

Please note this list identifies only some of the United States's leading trade shows, however there are many more trade shows available to retailers. For a more complete listing of shows, visit the below websites.

Advanstar | www.advanstar.com
Emerald Expositions | www.emeraldexpositions.com
Reed Expositions | www.reedexpositions.com
Tarsus Group | www.tarsus.com

In Chapter 5, we'll look at how you can maximize your trade show participation while also understanding how to prepare for trade shows and ways to follow up with vendors once the trade show has concluded. You will also gain a stronger understanding of how vendors affect your store story—for better or for worse.

Unique Traits of Your Store

Recognizing the importance of strong inventory assortment and how this shapes your merchant story is beneficial when preparing your communication plan with customers. Because consumers ultimately decide your success or failure as a merchant—after all, they either choose to shop at your store or not—it's important to factor them into your store's identity.

Nordstrom, an American upscale fashion retailer with over 250 locations, provides employees with one rule for all new hires. They simply state, "Use good judgment," followed by general legal and company expectations. This simple yet powerful plan for customer care has shaped Nordstrom to be recognized for top-notch customer service, stellar store reputation, and fantastic overall in-store experience. It's also a great example of a store from which independent retailers can learn.

RETAIL TIP

When creating your store story, consider how you *want* to be perceived by others. Now consider how you are *actually* perceived by others.

Wanting to be seen one way and actually being seen another way is a common scenario. Engage customers and potential customers alike via social media, focus groups, and surveys to understand their perception of your store. Ask questions, encourage feedback and comments, provoke conversation, and review what customers share with you. This will help you better understand the *reality* of how you are perceived versus the *idea* of how you think you are perceived.

Often independent retailers feel that because they can't offer comparable policies to those of big-box stores, they don't offer any at all. This can certainly create challenges, but rather than perceive this as an obstacle entirely, consider it a perk to being an independent merchant. As an independent retailer, you have the luxury to create your own rules, which also means setting your customer-care standards. Among these expectations should be identifying your store return policies, implementing checkout procedures, providing VIP customer standards, introducing store gift cards, and more.

Below, in no particular order, are various policies and procedures that all retailers should identify and use to shape their customer experience and overall store story.

Return Policies

First and foremost, it's vital to create a return policy that makes sense for the products you sell, as well as the customers you target. It is important to be realistic with your return-policy expectations while also being fair to your customers. For example, you could offer a store refund explicitly for returns made within 10 days of purchase. Or you could offer full refunds on items purchased and unused within 14 days of receipt date, but only with the receipt and delivered in the same payment form as the purchase was made. Once you have identified a policy that caters to your store's needs and clientele, post your policy within clear view of your checkout area, as well as including it on all receipts. Make it a habit to explain your return policy as part of your checkout procedure. One way to be sure that you never forget to do this is to have your customers initial the return-policy explanation on their receipt after you have explained it to them. This can help to alleviate difficult conversations with unhappy customers in the future. Finally, be sure to identify any limitations to your policy, such as certain vendors, defective items, or laws that may apply to products regarding "no-return policies."

Checkout Procedures

Everyone involved in the operation of your business should clearly understand all store policies, including those regarding the checkout procedure. This is a strong, if not the only, opportunity to create a personal and memorable moment with your customer, and its significance cannot be overstated. It's vitally important to forge repeat-customer relationships at every turn, and there's no better way than through personal interaction. On the flip side, if not managed correctly, a negative checkout experience can cripple your chances of repeat customers regardless of the other factors.

Make it a habit to share news of upcoming store events, specials, promotions, or other store activities during the checkout process. Kindly ask if the customer would be interested in sharing his or her e-mail address for store updates (exclusively), or perhaps suggest that your customer might "like" your store's Facebook page (you do have one, right?). Finally, be sure you have a standard "Thank you for your purchase" in place as well. It can certainly be customized to your store's personality, but everyone involved should be on the same page regarding the message you deliver. It is stunning how few times I actually see this done well in the independent community.

VIP Customer Care

No matter what kind of merchant you are, identifying your top customers should be a priority. Whether you sell $1 candy bars or $10,000 dresses, make it a point to track your strongest customers. Many point-of-sale (POS) systems can help you identify customers and their spending, but some independent retailers find success in managing VIP customers the old-fashioned way—taking note of purchases made, their birthdays, special occasions, and other reasons unique to the business. When identifying how you can better support this crowd, consider offering special events uniquely for them, providing distinctive services above and beyond your normal customer care—such as free home delivery or complimentary gift sending—as well as writing handwritten thank-you notes after each purchase they make. This type of customer care lets your VIPs know that you truly value their commitment to your store.

Store Gift Certificates

The National Retail Federation reports that 81 percent of shoppers in the 2012 holiday season bought at least one gift card. Although the holidays are not 365 days a year, birthdays and other special occasions are. With this in mind, make sure that you offer gift certificates to sell no matter what time of year it is. Not only will this increase your sales, but it also will likely introduce new customers to your store that you normally wouldn't have. The opportunity to sell *more* than the value of the gift card, referred to as an *uplift*, is also there—increasing your chances of a higher sale. Paper gift certificates versus plastic gift cards are easy to customize, allowing you to quickly introduce this to your store. Plastic gift cards can be easily customized as well, with such places as CardPrinting.us and PlasticResource.com both able to make gift cards specifically for your store. The key to managing a gift-card program is to create an easy-to-track system of when gift certificates are sold and redeemed. You can do this the old-fashioned way through pen and paper, but with today's POS systems, this can be managed much more effectively.

Store Hours

Customers do not shop at a store *solely* because they like it. Often they shop at a store *strictly* because the store accommodates their schedule. This means that if you close at 5 pm to rush home, potential consumers who only shop after their workday ends at 5 pm will never be your customers. When identifying your store hours, consider what most of the retailers in your community's hours are, what your immediate retail neighbors' hours are, any mandated hours applied by your city, and when your local customers generally shop. Tourist towns will vary from downtown corporate settings to Main Streets in small towns across the United States. Although there's no black-and-white schedule that is ideal for everyone, it's important to identify hours that accommodate your local customers and complement other merchants. Also, remember that closing your store one or two days a week isn't always an option. Keep your customers in mind—not your own personal schedule—when establishing your store hours, and you will be more likely to find a schedule that attracts more business.

Customer-Dispute Scenarios

When a customer is upset about your store's return policy, customer service, lack of inventory, store hours, or anything else, what matters most is how you handle it. Despite their often rude or inappropriate behavior, remain calm, and allow the customer to share his or her thoughts on the situation. Once the customer has said what he or she wants to, gently respond with your resolution. Avoid allowing the customer to see you get angry or heated, even if you are scream-ing inside. If your resolution does not make the customer happy, consider offering him or her a store gift certificate for $5, $10, or $25, and apologize that you cannot do anything more. The cost of giving the customer money to spend in your store is often a lot less than having the customer bad mouthing you for years to come.

Store Traditions

Annual sales, signature mints, festive occasions—big or small retail-ers should strive to be known for a handful of things that make them unique. Taking 10 percent off everything in your store on a random Saturday won't do the trick. Instead, seek out both small and large opportunities to make your store memorable. It may be the disco soundtrack that's always on repeat, the signature scent that customers instinctively remember your store by, an annual Christmas-in-July sale that has your employees dressing like elves, or a private red-carpet VIP event that gets your best customers excited every year. Whatever your unique somethings are, make them consistent, make them memorable, and make them worth talking about. All store characteristics will affect your overall suc-cess or failure, but it's often these little things that add up the most.

Store Staff

Shaping your story would not be complete without identifying the faces that make up your retail business. Your employees are a reflection of your store brand and therefore need to be carefully selected before welcoming them to your sales floor. Nowadays, an affordable part-time sales clerk is easy to find. What's not easy is finding a sales clerk worth having on your sales floor. Take the time to interview potential candidates with a series of interviews, and be sure to seek references from previous employers. Retail-Minded.com offers templates to help you track your interview process and provides employee review forms for when you have your staff in place. Below you can find some useful questions to help you navigate your next round of interviews.

General Interview Questions for Potential Employees

1. What were your major responsibilities at your last two jobs?
2. Which of your previous jobs did you like the most, and why? Which job have you had that you liked the least?
3. What has been your most rewarding experience at work?
4. What do you find most satisfying about working with others?
5. What was your single most important accomplishment for the company in your last job?
6. Why did you leave Company X?
7. If you could take with you one thing from your last company and bring it to this job, what would it be, and why?
8. What was the toughest problem you had to solve at a previous job, and how did you solve it?

9. Why do you want to work for this company?

10. After hearing a description of this position, why do you think you would be a good fit?

11. Do you have any reservations about any of the responsibilities identified in this role?

12. What skills did you learn in previous roles that you can use here?

13. What skills or experience do you think make you stand out from other candidates?

14. Where do you professionally want to be five (or ten) years from now?

15. Are there any other points you'd like to share with us about why you would make a good [insert job title here]?

Manager/Key-Holder Questions

1. How would you describe your management style?

2. What do you believe to be the most difficult role of a manager?

3. Many of our employees have been here for a while. How do you feel you can earn their respect as a manager?

4. What have you learned from other managers you have worked under in the past?

5. Who was your favorite manager, and why? Who was your least favorite manager, and why?

6. What do you think is the most important trait of successful managers?

7. If I were to ask someone who you previously managed your top three qualities as a manager, what do you think he or she would say?

8. If I were to ask that same person your three worst qualities, what do you think he or she would say?

9. Why do you like being a manager?

10. How would you plan to engage employees to work effectively under your leadership?

11. Do you consider employee morale part of your responsibilities? Why or why not?

12. Explain your most difficult management experience to date.

13. As a manager, do you consider teaching part of your job?

14. How good are you at delegating responsibilities?

15. What other points can you share with us about why you would make a good manager?

Another point to consider is that while it may be easy to hire family or friends, it's possible a more skilled candidate is available and will aid your store more efficiently. As a general rule of thumb, consider all candidates—including family and friends—equally, and put each candidate through the same interview process. This will help you identify the best person to fill your store's needs.

Collectively, the preceding unique traits of your store can set you apart from your competition and help make your store memorable among customers. It's important that you also factor in the value of customer service during your entire in-store experience, recognizing that this will also set you apart from other retailers in either a positive or negative fashion.

Kirt Manecke, customer-service expert and author of the book, *Smile: Sell More with Amazing Customer Service*, believes that in order to truly make your store memorable among consumers, you should aim to deliver consistent, strong customer service every day:

Delivering amazing customer service on a consistent basis to each and every customer means that you are prepared. Your staff has been trained to deliver service and sales in a way that is efficient for your customers. While there will always be customers who have decreased attention, are in a hurry, or appear to be frazzled, you want to still aim to deliver strong customer care despite any customer scenario. One way to do this is by treating people like guests in your home. Just as you would greet someone at your door, you should smile and greet every customer with a warm "Hello" within two seconds of their entering your business. This sets the stage for a happy shopping experience for your customers because they feel welcome and they know that you are on top of your business. Surprisingly, however, many retailers fail to do this.

Engage your customer, ask questions, and listen. Know your products and your competition so that you can quickly and efficiently answer your customers' questions and objections and sell your products better than any website or other store can do. Aim to guide your customers to the best product that fits their needs and wants, and then respectfully ask for the sale. If you do these things and more, consumers *will* pay attention and not only return to your store but also tell their friends as well.[4]

Finally, remember to look outside your comfort zone in all your business responsibilities, including how you deliver customer service, who you hire, which trade shows you attend, and what your store policies are.

. . .

When you identify what traits matter most in your store, how you manage its perception, and ways in which you can stand out in the marketplace, you are more likely to succeed in retail. Furthermore, consumers will be more receptive to shopping at a store that takes the time to earn a consumer's trust and dollars by applying high standards. An additional perk is that during this process, you will also find consistency in your own actions and be able to better support your customers, your store team, and yourself in delivering a strong in-store experience.

In the chapters that follow, we'll take an even closer look at how each decision you make will affect your store's personality and how customers perceive your business.

Action Guide

Every store tells a story, and your story needs to be easily understood from both an internal and an external perspective. Internally, having an organized employee manual will offer you tremendous guidance in employee hiring and management. To get started, consider the following objectives to include in your manual. You may find that some are not necessary for your store, whereas other objectives that are not noted, are. The goal, however, is to create a manual that makes sense for your unique business.

Organize a binder that collectively represents your store employee manual based on the following suggestions. Even for a solo store owner with no additional staff, this exercise will provide you with a foundation to keep your store operations and expectations in order. In addition, if a last-minute hire is ever needed, you will have a clear, concise manual to help you train that person in store support.

Although this exercise will take some commitment and time, it is a retail necessity worth investing your time in.

1. **Store contact details**
   a. Physical address
   b. E-mail
   c. Telephone
   d. Fax
   e. Web
   f. Social media accounts
2. **Store hours**
3. **Company philosophy**
4. **Employment practices**
   a. Equal employment opportunity statement
   b. Drug-free statement
   c. Harassment policy
   d. At-will statement
      i. Full-time employees
      ii. Part-time employees
      iii. Temporary/seasonal employees

    iv. Interns

5. **Termination statement**

    a. Voluntary

    b. Involuntary

6. **Operation procedures**

    a. Pay schedule

        i. Commission

        ii. Direct deposit

    b. Staff schedule

        i. Overtime

        ii. Tardiness

        iii. Absenteeism

        iv. Schedule changes

    c. Store opening and closing procedures

        i. Cash drawer details

        ii. POS and computer details

    d. Merchandising

        i. Display units

        ii. POS area

        iii. Floors

        iv. Shelves

        v. Other areas

7. **Customer-service expectations**

    a. Customer greetings

    b. General customer support

    c. Suggestive selling

    d. Customer management

    e. Telephone procedures

    f. Customer complaints

8. **External relationships**
   a. Vendors
   b. Shipping
   c. Trade/miscellaneous
9. **Emergency procedures**
10. **Security**
    a. Personal belongings
    b. Law enforcement contact details
    c. First aid box
11. **Dress code**
    a. Wardrobe
    b. Personal appearance
12. **Miscellaneous**
    a. Food and drink
    b. Personal phone use
    c. Cigarette smoking
    d. Computer use
    e. Nonemployee access
    f. Confidentiality

Make sure to save your employee manual to a Word file for easy editing. Furthermore, it's always a good idea to have all new employees review the manual and sign a statement acknowledging that they have done so. Finally, although a manual is not a legally binding contract, it never hurts to have an attorney review what you have created to ensure that you are accurately and legally supporting your store team.

PART II

Practical Steps to Increase Your Store Visibility and Sales

5

Sourcing Products Through Trade Shows and the Internet

Whether it's Google or Apple or free software, we've got some fantastic competitors, and it keeps us on our toes.

—*Bill Gates (1955–present), investor, entrepreneur, philanthropist*

As A retailer, there are countless external business resources that you will need to work with to run your business effectively. Among them are service providers, wholesalers, manufacturers, and distributors. This collective crowd of business resources offers retailers various ways to purchase and ultimately sell products through their stores. The question is: What makes sense for your business? To begin, however, you must first understand the differences among certain supplier sourcing strategies—and how ultimately each of these affects retailers.

Sourcing, as defined by Wikipedia.org, refers to "a number of procurement practices, aimed at finding, evaluating, and engaging suppliers of goods and services." Essentially, sourcing represents the act of finding products from wholesalers or manufacturers to resell through a business. In your case, this would mean reselling through your retail store.

In previous years, sourcing was not as accessible to retailers and, as a result, not used for their businesses on a routine scale. Nowadays, however, sourcing is readily available thanks to websites such as TopTenWholesale.com and Manufacturer.com, as well as events that include Sourcing at MAGIC and Source Direct at ASD—each held biannually in Las Vegas. These events are simultaneously held during MAGIC Market Week and the ASD Show, respectively, offering retailers a chance to engage with traditional vendors and wholesalers while also having the chance to meet importers, distributers, product-development teams, and other product professionals within the sourcing arena at each individual show.

Benefits of Sourcing as a Retailer

For retailers, there are many benefits to sourcing your own products for your store. Among them are saving valuable inventory and operating dollars by cutting costs of product purchases, gaining the ability to expand your store product base, offering diversification among your current supply chain, meeting new providers otherwise not available to you locally or even domestically, and learning how business is conducted in other cultures.

Megy Karydes, a former retailer and current writer and marketing consultant who works with small-business owners and organizations through her business, Karydes Consulting, encourages retailers to differentiate their stores through sourcing. She shares below some tips based on her own firsthand experience to help retailers navigate their sourcing journey:

One way to differentiate your retail business from others is to offer products straight from the source. Since many retailers are intimidated by sourcing—thinking it's too hard or unavailable to them—those who do realize greater margins, richer merchandising selections, and stronger relationships with their customers as a result of their sourcing finds, have a lot to gain that other merchants miss out on.

For those interested in testing the waters, my advice to you is to visit local art centers or smaller art fairs to identify items that might work for your store. I also encourage you to engage in dialogue with the artists to see if they'd be willing to create some pieces for your store. If your community doesn't have art fairs or anything of the sort, go online and check out sites such as Etsy, where you can reach out directly to the artists and ask them if they'd consider working with you.

Once you have identified someone to work with, the key is to create a mutually beneficial relationship. If the person feels that you're trying to take advantage of him or her, that person may work with you once but never again. Ideally, however, you should set a goal of developing a long-term relationship to help aid both you and your contact. To do this, I suggest that you invest some time at the onset working out the details, especially if the person isn't experienced working with wholesale customers. Spend some time to create a document for both of you to sign that outlines the following details. Essentially, this will act as a contract to ensure that you both meet the expectations identified on both sides of the business. You will not want to neglect the following points when developing this document:

- Pricing
- Exclusivity
- Packaging
- Merchandising
- Delivery details
- Payment schedule
- Unsold items
- Damaged items
- Length of contract

As a reminder, this document is intended to support your relationship and keep you on track in working terms. While friendly, verbal agreements always seem solid to start, but it's simply impossible to predict the future; and therefore, binding documents are a smarter way to manage your business.[1]

Karydes makes some fantastic points for you to consider, particularly as you attempt to try sourcing with baby steps before making a larger commitment. She extends her support with the following details for retailers considering how international sourcing can help their businesses:

Savvy retailers also know that talent extends beyond the pond. While sourcing internationally comes with its own sets of challenges, it's actually much easier than most people think. The Internet is a great resource when it comes to finding products all over the world, but if you're really looking to carry products from a specific country, start your research by finding the nearest embassy or consulate office, and let them know that you're interested in finding products from their country. While this isn't always the case, many of those offices have divisions that cover international trade and can be tremendously helpful with rules, regulations, contacts, and sources. Many even have funds in their budgets to fly buyers to the country to aid in buying trips, and it's worth asking if this is something they offer.

One of the questions I'm often asked about working with international suppliers and importing is how to deal with U.S. Customs. It's true that anytime you import, you'll have to declare what you're bringing in; and depending on what it is, also the country from which it's coming and the value of it as well. Furthermore, you may have to pay duties; but if you use a reputable customs broker or freight forwarder, often they will handle the paperwork to help you pass your items through customs. If you use services such as DHL or Federal Express, those companies will handle clearance for you. Shipping prices will vary considerably depending on what you're bringing in and which service you use. The more you import, the better you'll get at determining your best and least expensive shipping options.[2]

While venturing into the world of sourcing may seem like an intimidating task for retailers who have not explored this avenue yet, this doesn't have to be the case. Here are 10 tips to help further support you as you explore how sourcing may be right for your retail business:

1. Attend a wholesale market or trade show that has a sourcing section, allowing you to meet suppliers first-hand. This face-to-face opportunity will offer an educational experience for you, letting you engage and seek support to help you achieve your sourcing goals. Don't be afraid to speak up, either, during these opportunities. Ask questions, seek answers, listen carefully, and learn as much as you can from these sourcing professionals.

2. Visit an international sourcing provider or section of a trade show, such as Sourcing at ASD, to help expand your understanding of the vast range of sourcing opportunities for retailers. For some merchants, international providers may not be ideal for their brand messaging or store product assortment, but for others, this may be the perfect match for your business. Either way, understanding how international sourcing can aid your retail needs is something you should add to your sourcing to-do list.

3. Navigate the Internet to learn more about sourcing, as well as to get introduced to sourcing providers. This said, it's best not to solely go this route and eliminate actual trade show and sourcing event participation. Although the Internet can connect you to providers, it's important to consider all avenues of sourcing before making your final decision.

4. When seeking suppliers, get at least five quotes from different sellers to ensure that you are receiving the best

service, product, and deal possible. Seeking both domestic and global quotes can offer you a broader perspective on what may be best for your sourcing needs.

5. As you seek quotes from suppliers, be sure to identify the variations in minimum order quantities. These numbers can make a huge difference in the overall cost for you; therefore, you should seek a variety of quantity costs to help you to identify the best strategy for spending your allocated sourcing dollars.

6. Network with sourcing professionals, as well as work to build solid, good-standing relationships with your sourcing contacts. As in most industries, professionals in niche markets are likely to best support their clients when they are invested in caring for their actual success. For sourcing specifically, you can benefit from professionals "in the know" who may hear of something on a future date or know someone who knows someone who can help you in your sourcing needs.

7. Subscribe to sourcing-specific newsletters and trade magazines to continually learn and gain sourcing news. Among the best resources to do this is by subscribing for a free e-newsletter from TopTenWholesale.com as well checking out SourcingJournalOnline.com. In addition, we have identified some other key resources in the first sidebar in this chapter.

8. Continually research innovative trends and tactics specific to your product needs. Attending trade shows, visiting online sourcing sites such as TopTenWholesale.com, and referencing industry publications can all help you do this,

yet it's up to you to identify the need to constantly want to follow through. In other words, don't ever settle for what you currently do or what is currently offered. As time progresses, new ways to source and develop product will arise. Be sure to embrace these changes to help your business stay current and possibly even save money.

9. Know what your budget is before committing to a sourcing quote or quantity. There are a lot of costs incurred in retail and wholesale alike, and knowing what your budget is up front will help you to make better decisions. Also, do not let a limited budget hold you back from seeking sourcing opportunities. This simply means that you need to be that much more educated on where every dollar you spend goes.

10. Plan ahead for unexpected costs and challenging moments—if not days or months. This is not intended to scare or shy you away from sourcing but rather to prepare you for the realities of any new entrepreneurial adventure. As you seek to do something you have never done before, you should always expect that the excitement and good that come from this will also bring you hardships and uncertainties. This is simply part of the ride. Remember to lean on the vast range of resources available to you to help you in your sourcing journey and to stay on track with your budget and ultimate sourcing goals.

As you can see, there is an abundance to be learned about sourcing, and we encourage you to further expand your knowledge on this subject by reading Jason A. Prescott's book, *Wholesale 101: A Guide to Product Sourcing for Entrepreneurs and Small Business Owners* (McGraw-Hill, 2013).

SOURCING NEWS RESOURCES

Blog.trade.gov   Tradeology is the official blog of the International Trade Administration, which discusses international trade laws and other relevant industry news.

Manufacturing.net   Shares manufacturing industry-related news, trends, resources, and more related to the global manufacturing community.

Nam.org   A newsroom hosted by the U.S. National Association of Manufacturers sharing manufacturing related news.

RetailMinded.com   A retail-specific website that covers all aspects of running a retail business, including working with wholesalers and suppliers, as well many other key areas of retail. Offers free newsletter and subscription-based digital or print quarterly magazine.

SourcingJournalOnline.com   A global news resource with information for business executives and retailers who want to know more about supply-chain-related topics within the soft goods and textile industry.

TopTenWholesale.com   Covers wholesale industry news related to topics including vendor, supplier and wholesaler profiles, product news, trade show details, and more.

Working with Wholesalers

Similar to sourcing and typically more understood by retailers is wholesale, which—very simply—represents the sale of merchandise to retailers. On a more detailed level, wholesale represents the sale of products and goods to business owners, creating a business-to-business transaction versus a business-to-consumer transaction. As with sourcing, retailers have access to wholesalers through a variety of avenues, including trade shows, online platforms, and retail trade publications. Even more so than sourcing, however, retailers have the opportunity to work within some very specialized markets of wholesale. An example of this would be the Outdoor Retailer Show (www.outdoorretailer.com), which caters specifically to retailers seeking merchandise for outdoor sports for both summer and winter markets. Shows that cater to niche markets, such as outdoor sporting retailers, offer a tremendous value to merchants, specifically by

1. Introducing industry-specific brands and products directly to retailers
2. Sharing latest industry news and buzz through education, networking, and other face-to-face events
3. Demonstrating products for retailers to try hands on, allowing merchants to know firsthand what may be best for their businesses

In addition, retailers have access to countless trade shows that offer more expansive product assortments. An example of this would be the ASD Show, held biannually in Las Vegas, which attracts over 2,800 vendors per show and over 40,000 attendees per each event. The general merchandise assortment of wholesalers includes jewelry, souvenirs, toys, hobby, beauty, cosmetics, floral, gift, home decor, grocery, apparel, accessories, stationery, and much, much more. As a result, retailers have a one-stop-shop destination to seek a variety of products for their stores. Another fantastic trade show that caters to an expansive marketplace is the National Hardware Show, which attracts over 27,000 attendees seeking to learn, source, and connect specifically for the U.S. home-improvement and do-it-yourself (DIY) markets.

For merchants, it is important to identify how both niche-market trade shows and more diverse at-large shows can benefit their businesses. Typically, it's ideal to make attending both types of shows a priority. The reason for this is very simple: without doing this, you limit your exposure to potential brands, products, and resources that can add value to your store. Furthermore, by diversifying your buying experiences, you also set yourself apart from your competition. Attending niche-market shows only can limit you to products and wholesalers that your competition is likely buying from as well. However, if you introduce a show such as the ASD Show to your buying rotation, you will undoubtedly be able to incorporate inventory that your competitor doesn't also have. Specifically, you can narrow down your buying needs at shows such as the ASD Show for add-on sales, lower-priced products, and other unique items to complement your category-specific purchases from your niche-market trade show. These shows, however, such as the Consumer Electronics Show (CES)—held annually in Las Vegas—will always remain destinations that retailers can't miss.

Understanding the Value of Trade Shows

Scheduling trade shows into your operational calendar is an important responsibility to constantly keep up with, particularly when you should plan for an assortment of trade shows to attend each year. As a retailer, it's nearly impossible to effectively run your store without attending trade shows; therefore, knowing how to maximize your time spent per show is extremely important. Furthermore, because it costs money to travel to trade shows, you want to ensure that you are maximizing your investment in each event you attend.

In no particular order, here are eight reasons you should make trade shows a priority on your operational calendar. Not only will you be able to gain tips on strengthening your trade show experiences through the identified points, but you should also be able to justify the value in why trade shows are an important experience for any retail business.

1. Trade shows allow you to gain knowledge about and exposure to new trends, products, and resources. The combination of wholesalers, suppliers, distributors, and vendors is a great way to learn about what's hot, what's fading, and what your company needs to introduce into its store in the seasons ahead.

2. Trade shows stimulate new ideas and creative ways to support your business through aspects that expand beyond inventory alone. This includes offering retailers exposure to companies that support in-store operations, providing trade show attendees with educational oppor-

WHOLESALE MARTS & BUYING DISTRICTS

Across the United States are a variety of wholesale marts and buying districts that cater to retailers all year long. While they are not officially considered trade shows, they are very similar in their services by offering a destination for retailers to connect with suppliers. Below are some of the wholesale marts and buying districts we recommend visiting in the United States.

America's Mart | Atlanta, GA | www.americasmart.com

Midwest Market Days | Chicago, IL | www.midwestmarketdays .com

The Dallas Market Center | Dallas, TX | www.dallasmarketcenter .com

The Miami Merchandise Mart | Miami, FL | www.miamimerchandisemart.com

The Wholesale District in Los Angeles | Los Angeles, CA | www .fashiondistrict.org

The World Market Center | Las Vegas, NV | www.wmclv.com

In addition, there are many other marts in cities nationwide that may be more ideal based on your geographic location. Finally, New York City offers many merchandise and garment districts that can be identified at the website below:

www.nyc.com/visitor_guide/garment_district.75853/editorial_ review.aspx tunities, and offering show participants networking and social experiences. Collectively, these all add value to your business.

3. Trade shows provide a meeting spot for retailers and vendors to connect face to face. Because it's nearly impossible for most wholesale representatives to travel to each individual retail account they have, a trade show becomes an ideal spot for them to connect with retailers. These events allow retailers to see a wholesaler's entire inventory assortment while also providing a venue for them to engage in person.

4. Trade shows give you the chance to generate leads for future vendor and product opportunities. As a merchant, you can never be too sure what the future will bring, and therefore, it's essential to have an idea of other brands, products, and businesses that may be able to aid you in future buys or store changes. To help prepare you for scenarios like this, collect business cards, keep trade show directories, and organize collected line sheets and other product details to refer to should you need to get in touch with these companies once the trade show has ended and before the next one begins.

5. Trade shows offer educational experiences that can only be found at these events, eliminating your chance to gain these experiences otherwise. One example of this is the Independent Retailer Conference held at the ASD Show in Las Vegas, which introduces a select group of industry experts and business resources for show attendees to engage with and learn from. Through various seminars, as well

as four days of face-to-face opportunities for merchants and these select retail leaders to connect, show attendees can gain an abundance of knowledge to take back to their stores. Furthermore, their participation in these education-rich experiences is often free to show attendees—something any budget-strapped retailer can appreciate.

6. Trade shows allow you to get answers right away, offering an immediate communication platform through which retailers and show exhibitors can connect. To help aid you in gaining the information you want to know, it's always a good idea to come prepared to a trade show with written questions and ideal goals you want to accomplish during your trade show visit.

7. Trade shows offer you the chance to connect with like-minded retailers who may not be your direct competitors. An example of this would be if you connected with a retailer from a state on the other side of the country who has a store similar in inventory assortment to yours. The value in this is that you can lean on each other as retail professionals yet not feel threatened by sharing a local marketplace. Moreover, when you have like-minded retail friends, you can trade or sell your inventory with one another if one of you is having more success with a certain product than another. Allowing yourself to meet retailers and engage with them is also a great way to realize that you aren't alone in your retail journey, and even as an independent merchant, you don't have to make every decision by yourself. Leaning on like-minded retailers helps to eliminate this isolated mind-set.

8. Trade shows give you a chance to have fun. Yes, you read that right—have fun! Nothing gives a business owner more energy and the desire to work more than having a good time while working. Trade shows certainly introduce long days and information overload, but they also strengthen and refresh a retailer's motivation to work hard, work smarter, and create more success for their stores.

While realizing the benefits of trade shows, retailers should also never underestimate the value of planning ahead before attending one. Camille Candella, group marketing manager of Emerald Expositions, believes that "whether you are a seasoned pro or new to trade shows, you should always do your homework prior to arriving at a show. You want to maximize your time at the show, and that means preparing in advance."[3]

To help you do this, we encourage you to learn as much as you can about a trade show prior to attending it. Using online resources and any registration materials received, become familiar with show exhibitors, special events, education experiences, and the entire show agenda prior to arriving at the show. This allows you to plan in advance what is a priority for you to accomplish, as well as identify general time allowances you will need. It's also very important to take the time to pack well for your trade show trip. This means packing comfortable shoes because most trade shows entail a lot of walking. You should also plan for a comfortable bag to carry with you throughout your trade show visit, allowing room to hold collected line sheets, buyer packets, promotional giveaways, business cards, and more. Don't forget to pack your own business cards as well. Another tip includes checking whether the trade show you are attending allows for bags with wheels. Many retailers find that a mini suitcase or briefcase on wheels is ideal for trade shows, but some shows do not allow these on their floors because of limited space. Finally, bringing along a mini stapler, pens, filing folders, and other organizational products often can help you to better manage the paperwork you collect at the trade show.

Managing Orders Placed at Shows

Whether you have attended countless trade shows or have yet to visit your first, among the most important responsibilities you have in managing your trade show experience is dealing with orders placed while at the show. For retailers who have previously placed orders while attending a trade show: Did you do a good job in effectively spending your open-to-buy (OTB) dollars and staying within budget? Were the orders you placed received on time and according to the terms identified when you placed them? Did you feel supported by the companies from which you ordered following the show?

There are many questions retailers should ask themselves with regard to product management, trade show effectiveness, and their overall retail business. Ultimately, the questions you want to challenge yourself with should direct you to managing your store more effectively for you—not the wholesaler, supplier, distributor, or other product professional with whom you are working. Although it's important to consider both sides of these business relationships, it's critical to continually evaluate whether the decisions you are making for your store are the best ones you can make.

To help accomplish this goal, be sure you stay within your identified budget when placing orders at trade shows. Often all types of domestic and international suppliers will offer you show specials to increase your enthusiasm to buy more from them. Certainly these specials can offer you many perks and savings, but don't lose sight of the budget you have to work with. Moreover, don't neglect your target shipping dates, product deliveries, minimum order ideals, payment terms, and other buying factors that matter to you. In many cases, simply communicating with your vendor contact is all it takes to shift what he or she is offering to what you actually need.

EXPERT SPOTLIGHT

Bob Berg, director of sales of International Business at the Sourcing at MAGIC trade show, believes there are three must-know tips for retail attendees to follow when they participate at any trade show.

1. Have a clear understanding of what your goal is at the show. Remind yourself of this goal as each day passes to ensure you stay on track.

2. Organize yourself prior to the show. Identify exhibitors you hope to see, schedule vendor appointments, plan for events or other extra activities, and identify any marketing materials you may want to have available with you at the trade show. These may include business cards or other promotional items.

3. Give yourself time to navigate the trade show without feeling rushed. By taking shortcuts, squeezing in appointments, and skipping vendors, you miss opportunities for your business.

Retailers often feel rushed and stretched for time while at trade shows, letting themselves make quick decisions as a result. To the best of your ability, you should avoid doing this in all situations—most important, though, when you are about to write an order. Having a prewritten checklist of your ideal order terms—not just your ideal products—can help you to stay on track with your shipping, delivery, payment, and other order goals. Furthermore, remember that vendors create order terms to their benefit—not yours. With this in mind, do not hesitate to speak up regarding their identified terms and let them know your preferred terms if they vary. Although the vendor ultimately has the final call here, communicating your preferred delivery dates, product needs, and other order details is to your benefit. What is also to your benefit is to actually place orders at the shows you attend in an effort to gain show specials offered by vendors that may save you money.

Finally, make sure that you have your store's tax ID number, shipping address, and company contact details readily available for you to provide to vendors as you write orders at shows. If you have a premade sticker, stamp, or business card with all these details on it, this can save you time during the order-writing process. Many vendors still input order details by pen and paper despite the advanced technology available, so don't be surprised if this occurs.

* * *

Incorporating trade shows into your retail calendar is one of the most important steps you can take as an independent retailer. The experiences trade shows offer you, as well as the opportunity to meet suppliers, distributors, vendors, wholesalers, and other industry professionals, can't be matched by any other industry experience. Just remember that vendors at trade shows are there to sell, whereas retailers are there to both research and buy—two very different things. Although vendors and retailers complement each other, be sure that you stay focused on the goals you have set for your business versus altering them for theirs. Ultimately, this will keep you on the path to having success in each of your trade show journeys.

Using Online Sourcing Platforms

While trade shows will always remain an important destination for you to acquire inventory for your store, the Internet has made it possible for you to connect with vendors, manufacturers, suppliers, and other product professionals as well. Often this is a great destination to kick-start your product research, with online sites being readily available to you at all hours of the day and night. Searching for your specific product on Google, Yahoo, or Bing can be challenging, however, and you should keep in mind that a search engine is only as good as what it indexes based on a special algorithm. Many suppliers and overseas factories do not have great websites, thus making it hard to find them through these search engines. Fortunately, however, you can gain quick access to supplier information when using keyword searches on online business-to-business (B2B) platforms that are trusted and secure.

The best way to ensure that you are working with a secure, credible B2B platform when sourcing online is to identify that it is well known, respected, and has reliable suppliers within its network. In the United States, these include:

- TopTenWholesale.com
- Manufacturer.com
- MFG.com
- Modalyst.co
- Thomasnet.com
- WholesaleCrafts.com

Retailers open to working with business trade platforms based in China and Asia include:

- Made-in-china.com
- GlobalSources.com
- IndiaMART.com

As you explore additional online B2B platforms, it's likely that you will run into websites that advertise hidden supplier lists or want to charge you a fee. Generally speaking, you should be wary of these sites because most of them are scams. As a retailer, you can gain supplier, wholesaler, and vendor information for free—never having to pay for these details. The way that credible online marketplaces make money is from their advertisers and actual suppliers profiled, not from the retailers who use the platforms to buy and source for their stores. This is an important detail to remember because, unfortunately, there seems to be an increasing number of scammers out there looking to gain money from retailers via this avenue.

RETAIL TIP

When attending trade shows, don't underestimate the value of the educational opportunities available to you. Most nationally based trade shows and even select regional market centers offer education resources that are intended to help their attendees advance in their retail goals. Taking the time to learn from the retail leaders selected to deliver presentations, workshops, seminars, and other learning opportunities at these events are key experiences that can help your business thrive. Also, these often provide you the chance to connect one on one with industry experts prior to or after their presentations. These types of opportunities are nearly impossible to create solely for yourself, therefore, taking advantage of these events is yet another reason not to miss trade shows.

To help further ensure that you can trust online marketplaces and sourcing platforms, make sure that there is a phone number associated with the company. Typically, this should direct you to a support center for the company's platform, but at the very least, it should direct you to a live person who can answer any questions you may have. Next, you want to trust that the suppliers identified on these websites are safe. Reputable companies that offer you online supplier information will always offer you the chance to review their verification process, and you should never hesitate to ask about this if you have any questions. Another tip to consider is whether or not the representatives of the B2B platform you are reviewing attend trade shows. By actually participating in trade shows, you can trust that they are truly engaged within their niche-market networks and work with suppliers identified on their sites firsthand. Finally, while you should never have to pay any fees, you want to make sure that the profiled suppliers do pay. This means that they are benefiting from the platform and find value in it.

RETAIL TIP

Online B2B platforms are extremely valuable to retailers since they are available to be reviewed 24/7. Another online destination that can help you manage your business is the Resource Guide from Retail Minded. This online directory is a free resource published annually for merchants to gain trusted, reliable information on businesses that support retailers in their store operations. Unlike B2B platforms, this directory is solely focused on businesses that cater to the operations of running a retail store. Categories included in Retail Minded's Resource Guide include e-mail marketing, in-store media, inventory management, employee payroll, retail packaging, in-store signage, and more. To download a free copy of this directory, simply visit http://retailminded.com/resource-guide/.

Finally, to assist you in further exploring online sourcing for your retail store, we've taken a closer look at the leading B2B platform TopTenWholesale.com and identified what it can offer you. Operating with the tagline, "Find it. Source it. Profit!" the company's search engines and directory network offer you the ability to interact with thousands of wholesalers and manufacturers. The company's core concentration of product focuses on general merchandise, welcoming retail buyers from a vast range of retail categories. These include over 100 product categories and over

RETAIL TIP

Below is an example of a website page from TopTenWholesale .com, where you can source thousands of vendors for your retail store. Their extensive range of product sources, as well as trade show partnerships, help you effectively identify what the right mix of inventory may be for your store shelves.

1 million products—totaling an impressive number of over 35,000 suppliers for you to source from.

As with most B2B platforms, you will need to register on Top-TenWholesale.com to gain access to all its resources, although many are available for free without ever registering at all. The benefit of this, however, is that you can create a profile and manage your account, as well as adjust your privacy settings to your preferences. Senior business manager Jonathan Prescott at JP Communications, Inc., had this to say about TopTenWholesale.com:

> Buyers are able to save their favorite suppliers and products on TopTenWholesale.com, as well as connect directly with some of the largest manufacturers, importers, and distributors in the world. This offers a tremendous benefit to busy retailers because they can log on and off at their convenience. Furthermore, it's important to remember that sites like Top-TenWholesale.com simply connect buyers and sellers, and purchases being made are not being made through us directly. The perks of working with us, however, include an online chat feature known as Trade Chat—which is basically an instant messaging platform for buyers and sellers to quickly connect—as well as countless other features that allow you to manage your sourcing needs and unique retail goals.[4]

* * *

Identifying products that make sense for your store is often considered the most preferred responsibility of a retailer. With countless trade shows and online platforms available to help you do this, we hope that you will embrace the resources available to you in an effort to maximize your product-buying potential. In Chapter 6, we'll discuss how you can manage this inventory once it's received at your store, as well as ways in which you can help promote it and encourage sales in the later chapters.

Action Guide

Looking ahead over the next 12 months, identify no less than two trade shows that you want to attend. Focus on the following questions to help you plan for these events, with a core concentration on planning for how much it will cost you to attend.

* Where is the show?
* When is the show?
* How many days is the show offered?
* How many days do you believe you need to be on site at the show?
* Will you need to schedule additional days for travel?
* How much will airfare cost?
* Do the show dates overlap on days that you normally would be in your store?
* How many working hours will you need to budget for another employee to be at your store in your absence?
* Do you want to budget for an additional person to attend the show with you? If so, factor in the cost of that person's travel and, if necessary, working hours for which you will pay that person.

- Will this person need his or her own hotel room or can you share?
- Once at the show, will there be transportation costs to and from the hotel to the actual site?
- Does the show offer any special rates for hotel, airfare, taxis, or other accommodation details?
- What other costs might you incur by participating in a trade show, such as child care or other personal expenses?

Taking the time to answer these questions will allow you to look ahead at how much it will cost you to attend no less than two trade shows per year. Once you have identified a general amount to allocate for this, budget this into your store operations. By making this a priority and not an exception, you will be better positioned as a retailer.

6

Buying for Customers Versus Yourself

Your most unhappy customers are your greatest source of learning.

—*Bill Gates (1955–present), inventor, investor, philanthropist*

TIME AND time again we have found ourselves speaking with retailers and sharing stories about how their stores came to life. Many of these conversations begin with "I opened my store because I love [insert whatever it is you love here]." Whether it be shoes, fashion, home decor, surfing, animals, bikes, model airplanes, or anything else your heart may desire, we've heard it all when it comes to why folks of all ages and walks of life have ventured into the retail business.

Ironically, however, we rarely hear store owners telling us they opened their businesses because they love working with people.

The irony in this has always fascinated us and, we imagine, will continue to do so. It's quite possible that this exact reason, however, keeps us so inspired to help merchants better understand the business of retail as well as its greatest obstacle—consumers.

Understanding the Basics of Retail Math

"Each customer that walks through your door is voting with their dollars and telling you what they want you to have more of . . . and what they want you to have less of. You need to look at the decisions they are making through their purchases and evaluate it monthly," CEO and nationally recognized retail expert Cathy Wagner of RetailMAVENS explains.

EXPERT SPOTLIGHT

Taking an in-depth look at your inventory should always be on the top of your to-do-list. Retail expert Cathy Wagner of Retail-MAVENS shares five tips to help you manage your inventory with a goal of increasing sell-thru.

1. Look at the % of business done in the different classes of inventory of your store by dividing the amount of sales in each class by the total of sales (without sales tax).

(Sales by Class / Total Store Sales) X 100 = % of Sales by Class

2. Next look at the amount of inventory that you have in each class at retail. Divide the dollar amount of inventory of each class by the total inventory to determine what % of inventory each class represents.

(Inventory at Retail by Class / Total Store Inventory at Retail) X 100 = % of Inventory by Class at Retail

3. Compare the % of inventory to the % of sales for each class. The % of sales of a class should match the % of inventory that the class represents of the total inventory.

4. Make adjustments so that the % of the inventory of a class matches the % of the sales that the class represents. For example, if the inventory of a class is $5,000 out of $20,000, then it represents 25% of the entire inventory. If the sales of that class are 50% of the total sales, then you have to increase the inventory to 50% of the total inventory. Since the inventory is $20,000, we know that the retail inventory of the class must be brought to $10,000. This means you should then order more inventory.

5. While making adjustments like this, you will find that there is another class that represents a larger % of inventory than sales. Take action immediately to mark down whatever items are slowing that class down so that you can decrease the inventory accordingly.

Understanding your inventory and its performance is critical in gaining consumer attention and store sales. To help you do this, Wagner suggests reviewing each vendor or brand you carry in your store by dollars, not units. For example, if you received $1,000 in inventory (priced at retail, not wholesale) and after four months sold $200, still owning $800, then you would have a 20 percent sell-through (200/1,000). For most retailers, this is a bad scenario, suggesting that your inventory of choice was not well received by customers and therefore isn't selling to plan. The question then becomes: What do you do?

Wagner, a nationally recognized retail expert known for her expertise in inventory management specifically, offers the following advice:

Look at the percentage of business done in the different classes of inventory of your store versus strictly by vendor or brand. Next, look at the amount of inventory that you have in each class at retail. Divide the dollar amount of inventory of each class by the total to determine what percent of inventory each class represents. Finally, compare the percent of inventory to the percent of sales for each class. The percent of sales of a class should match the percent of inventory that the class represents of the total inventory. To help ensure that you fully understand this on a consistent basis, I suggest that you do this exercise monthly. Also, know that there are few exceptions to this scenario. This is an excellent way of listening to your customers and making sure that you are buying what your customers want you to carry—not just what you want to sell.[1]

Evaluating your existing inventory and vendor assortment is a responsibility that should never leave your to-do list. Often retailers get caught up in the habit of buying products they love but their customers ultimately do not; therefore, it can be a challenge to shift gears and make purchase decisions based on your actual sales or customer demands. Recognizing that your taste and the taste of your actual customers may vary can be challenging—yet accepting this is key.

RETAIL TIP

Running a retail store means more than just identifying a great assortment of inventory. It means doing a lot of math. Never go into a season without a completed open-to-buy (OTB) plan. Better yet, never go into a fiscal year without a full OTB plan set in place. Next, make sure you accurately identify your store's gross margin, return on investment, inventory turnover, net sales, sell-thru and stock-to-sales ratio using the retail formulas below.

Total Sales – Cost of Goods = Gross Margin

Gross Margin $ / Average Inventory Cost =
Gross Margin Return on Investment

Net Sales / Average Retail Inventory (Sku Count) =
Inventory Turnover

Gross Sales – Returns & Allowances = Net Sales

Units Sold / Units Received = Sell Through %

Beginning of Month Stock / Total Month Sales =
Stock-to-Sales Ratio

Once you realize that your personal taste, preferred purchases, or product picks aren't always the same as those of your customers, you will open yourself up to making purchases that are stronger suited for optimal sell-through. To help you accomplish this, analyze how much money you make per each vendor in your store per season. To do this, simply take the amount sold less the cost of the inventory and then divide that number by the amount sold and multiply that by 100. This will calculate the *maintained markup* (MMU) for that vendor.

Maintained markup (MMU) = (amount sold – cost)/amount sold × 100

Although your ideal MMU will vary based on your retail sector and average price points of inventory, typically you want to see your MMU at over 50 percent per vendor. You should consider eliminating vendors or specific products performing at less than 50 percent from your store assortment altogether after implementing a markdown strategy to help recover some of your investment into them. You also should consider increasing the total quantity of items that exceed 80 percent, which may include introducing more color assortments, a variety of styles, or deeper buys into whatever that item may be. As always, though, you will want to repeat your review of each vendor or specific item sell-through during and no later than at the end of each season to control your purchase quantities, as well as your overall open-to-buy (OTB) dollars.

OTB dollars = projected sales + projected markdowns + planned end-of-month inventory – planned beginning-of-month inventory

In addition to using strategic retail formulas to manage your inventory sell-through, consider introducing a customer focus group into your store buying agenda. Traditionally speaking, a focus group helps to deliver research by asking people questions regarding their opinions, perceptions, attitudes, and overall interests regarding a product, service, idea, or (in your case) store from a collective perspective. The value in incorporating a customer focus group into your store strategy is that you can gain firsthand realistic and informative insight to help you react more appropriately to your target consumer interests.

Introducing Customer Feedback for Inventory Management

Karen Hollis, an Illinois-based jewelry retailer who has had her own jewelry store since 2005, introduced a customer advisory board in early 2013. Ultimately, her goal was to have more in-depth conversations about her store experience and her store inventory during her customer advisory meetings. Choosing a midweek evening to bring a group of 20 customers together, Hollis created a relaxing environment that allowed customers to both have fun and share their thoughts on her store, K. Hollis Jewelers.

"I identified customers I felt knew my store well enough to comment on it," Hollis explained. Choosing customers who ranged from big spenders to moderate spenders allowed Hollis to gain a more diverse understanding of her store as well.

During this two-hour event, Hollis offered light appetizers and drinks, encouraging customers to walk around the store at their leisure. Hollis also incorporated fishbowl-style vases through-out the store and pieces of paper and pens for customers to share their thoughts on anything—whether it was to say they didn't like something or thought a certain category of product should be introduced. Hollis welcomed customers to share any insight that could help *her* to further help *them*.

By welcoming customers to speak up, get involved, and share their thoughts on your store inventory and other details about your store, you can learn more about what your customers *really* want. If hosting quarterly, biannual, or even once-a-year advisory board events is not in your forecast, make sure that you still welcome truthful feedback from consumers via comment cards and social media. Ask your customers directly for their thoughts about your store, identifying specific questions to help them respond to what you are most curious about. Indicating that you want to hear both pros and cons about your store can help customers to open up with their responses as well.

Some suggested questions to direct to customers via a customer advisory meeting, social media, or comment cards in your store include the following:

1. What is your favorite vendor and/or item currently sold in our store?
2. What is your least favorite vendor and/or item currently sold in our store?
3. Are there any vendors, products, or brands that we don't sell that you think we should? Please identify them.
4. What is your average budget when shopping for items that are part of our store assortment?

5. Did you buy something the last time you visited our store? Why or why not?

6. If today is your first time visiting our store, would you plan to visit again? Why or why not?

7. If you are a repeat customer, what reasons keep you returning to our store?

8. Do you have suggestions on how we can better support you in your purchasing decisions?

9. What other stores would you consider visiting instead of ours? Why?

10. Does our product assortment make you excited to make a purchase? Please explain.

Supporting the idea to solicit customer insight, Dr. Gary Edwards, chief customer officer at Mindshare Technologies, believes that speaking up is part of the job of a merchant. "If retailers don't ask, their customers won't tell—and what they don't know can hurt their business in numerous ways."[2]

Using the information you receive, create an action plan to better support your store buys as well as your store experience. Moreover, Dr. Edwards recommends checking out what your customers are saying on review sites such as Yelp.com and CitySearch.com, both of which highlight retail stores with customer reviews.

RETAIL TIP

Illinois-based retailer Tom Konopacki experienced a "seven-year itch" that pushed him to want more than just his single store, Anastazia, in Geneva, Illinois. His solution? Opening store number 2. While expanding his existing store was one idea, ultimately he decided a second location would allow him to reach more customers and gain more sales.

"A bigger store doesn't necessarily translate to twice as many sales. Instead, another location makes more sense."

Konopacki decided on opening a second store 26 miles from his original store in Glen Ellyn, Illinois. Ninety percent of his merchandise is duplicated, while the other 10 percent is distinctive to each respective store's customers and sales patterns.

"Adding a second location has resulted in nearly double annual revenue, but that comes with double rent, payroll, and inventory, as well. It's important that while we have similar inventory in our stores, we don't forget that each store has it's own core customer. I try to always cater to the actual customer at each store, and for us that means buying more impulse, gift-style buys at our Geneva store and larger furniture pieces for our Glen Ellyn location. Only 10 percent of the store inventory may vary, but that 10 percent adds up. Every percent does, actually, which is why I'm always evaluating our customers, our inventory, and what we can do better to increase business."[3]

Using Point-of-Sale Software to Help Manage Inventory

"Growing a business comes down to data. If you don't thoroughly understand how your business is performing, what your cash flow is like, and who your customers are, growing—and even just running—a business can be a real gamble,"[4] Vaughan Rowsell, Vend CEO, believes.

As Rowsell suggests, managing inventory demands precise care. Having strong point-of-sale (POS) software is a key factor in this equation, allowing retailers to confidently manage and track their inventory as well as their customer loyalty. Rowsell shares five reasons that retailers can benefit from incorporating a POS system into their store management. Specifically, the benefits identified can all be gained from Vend POS, whereas many also can be achieved via POS software from other providers.

> *Reason 1:* POS systems easily keep track of inventory and always know exactly how much inventory you have in stock.
>
> *Reason 2:* POS systems allow you to run reports on which products are selling, when they are selling, and how often, allowing you to gain a real understanding of your product turnover and busy period.
>
> *Reason 3:* POS systems offer retailers a way to understand their customers' preferences and spending habits by sharing actual data. As a result, merchants can create targeted marketing campaigns in response to these

data, strengthening their overall store management and marketing efforts.

Reason 4: Some POS systems (such as Vend) even have built-in loyalty programs, giving retailers tools to reward customers and encourage repeat business.

Reason 5: Good POS systems should keep your data safe. Excel files, paper notebooks, and spreadsheets are all well and good, but they aren't highly rated when it comes to longevity or security. It's easy to spill a cup of coffee on a notebook or a laptop and completely destroy hours (or years) worth of painstaking labor. Having a state-of-the-art POS system means safely and painlessly storing your information (including sales and daily reports) in the cloud so that you never lose it.[5]

In addition to the preceding reasons that POS systems are good for retailers, it's important to also consider which POS system is good specifically for *your* business.

Rowsell recommends taking the time to research which POS system provider makes the most sense for your unique retail store, allowing you to accurately understand all your options before making an investment in a POS system:

Write a list of all the features you need to have; then start searching, and stick to that list. This will help to prevent you from getting swept off your feet by the marketing glamour of all the solutions out there. Furthermore, once you've selected the right POS system, take the time and spend the money necessary to set up your POS properly from the

RETAIL TIP

Point-of-sale (POS) providers can streamline inventory management while also helping to support reasons for marketing, in-store events, customer loyalty, and more. The difference is all in the details, however. To ensure you select the right POS provider for your business, make sure you complete demonstrations of each POS provider you are considering, as well as identify if the POS software you are considering meets the needs of your business.

Below is an example of Vend's inventory management and product history specific to one unique item. One of the benefits of using a POS software like Vend is that you can extensively identify selling patterns, inventory challenges, and more through their expansive data details.

beginning. This will save you lots of time and heartache down the road."[6]

Finally, remember that combining your efforts to identify the best inventory assortment for your store is the ideal way to manage your inventory. "By utilizing all types of feedback, retailers increase their ability to listen to their customers and to improve their retail-consumer relationships,"[7] Dr. Edwards further explains.

Ultimately, you have control over how you spend your OTB dollars, but it is customers who really make the buying decisions. Don't neglect their voice in your inventory management, and in return, they will be less likely to neglect your store.

· · ·

In the chapters that follow, we'll discuss how you can better manage and market your inventory by introducing you to various businesses that can help as well as by providing tips you can apply to your store right away. Among these are in-store events and display pointers. We'll discuss how technology affects retailers today and whether or not mobile commerce has an effect on your business.

Action Guide

Retail expert and CEO of RetailMAVENS Cathy Wagner works with thousands of retailers, helping them to obtain retail profits. Her thought on managing your inventory and increasing your paycheck is that it requires the same strategy as eating an elephant. Yes, I said it, eating an elephant.

"Growing your business requires the same strategy as eating an elephant. An elephant is HUGE, and if I were going to eat it—what would I do? How would I start? Where would I start? There is a secret and super easy way to do it . . . one bite at a time,"[8] explains Wagner.

If your goal is to have a larger paycheck, the most important step you can take is to manage your single largest expense well. This means that you have to learn how to control your inventory better.

"The effort that you spend doing that yields such a large impact because cost of goods represents about 50 percent of your sales,"[9] Wagner further explains. Furthermore, this type of goal takes time to accomplish, which is no different than eating a huge elephant one bite at a time.

Here's an example: If you do $400,000 in business, you are spending about $200,000 on your inventory in a year. If you were buy one item that cost that much, think about how much research and effort you would put into making a good decision. However, too often buyers are guilty of spending $500 here and $1,200 there without knowing for sure if it is being spent where it should be. That should not happen—ever. Wagner's advice? "Take control of your inventory and start putting more dollars in your pocket."[10]

In following Wagner's advice, take the time to organize your inventory into classifications of inventory versus inventory by vendor. The following steps will show you how to do this and why this is valuable for your business:

1. *Group your store items by stock-keeping unit (SKU) into classifications of inventory—or classes—versus by vendor.* A class is a group of similar inventory—similar in type of item and inventory turn. By breaking your inventory down into manageable bite-sized pieces, it is easy to control. When you look at your store by classes, you can analyze sales and inventory levels better. And when that happens, it becomes easier to control. The result is increased growth in sales and profits.

2. *Give your customers what they want.* Customers tell us what they want every time they buy something from us. They are voting with each dollar they spend. When they make a purchase, they are voting that they want more of that class of items. Key point here: their purchase should represent a whole class of items, not just a single item. They are telling you that you do a good job buying dresses or candles or chairs. You have to look beyond the actual item itself, though. When you have classes, you can track what customers want from you and make sure that you have just enough for them, as well as an assortment to offer them. This knowledge gives you power in your retail buying.

3. *React to the classes being identified as top performers, as well as low performers.* Let's say that you want to increase your purchases for the holidays by 10 percent because you believe that your business will grow by that much. Just adding 10 percent across the board would be a big mistake. Retail spending is never evenly distributed among every class; therefore, your retail buys should

not be even either. Some classes will be up 20 percent, maybe even 25 percent, and some other classes should be down 15 percent. If you just added 10 percent to all your orders, you would end up overinventoried in some classes and underinventoried in others. Essentially, this would cause some of your customers to leave your store and shop elsewhere because you couldn't give them what they wanted. However, when you know the demand of each class, you can look at how each is trending and then buy accordingly.

Remember that inventory management is not something to occasionally do—but rather to always do. Make inventory management a top priority of your store to ensure strong sell-through and smarter buying decisions.

7

Selling Your Products

Obstacles don't have to stop you. If you run into a wall,
don't turn around and give up. Figure out how to climb it,
go through it, or work around it.

—*Michael Jordan (1963–present), former NBA player, entrepreneur*

ALTHOUGH BUYING inventory is an extremely important part of a retailer's job, the hardest part of all is still left ahead—selling what has been purchased. The dynamics that surround selling in brick-and-mortar retail storefronts are much greater and more diverse and extreme than at any other time in retail history. Often merchants feel bombarded with the various "new" technologies and other retail-focused products that are marketed to help them in their business operations. Furthermore, the core responsibilities of running a storefront, such as merchandising and tracking inventory, must remain top of mind for busy retailers despite the vast range of other responsibilities on their to-do lists. Combined, these responsibilities create a challenging agenda for retailers to manage, often resulting in overlooked or undermanaged situations.

Michael Amato, former president of Washington Mutual and current CEO and president of Cimarron, an advisory firm that helps leaders make their mark on their businesses, encourages retailers and all entrepreneurs to be strategic in their business operations. Amato explains:

> It's imperative for small-business owners to focus on strategic alignment. An entrepreneur should not only develop a vision and mission statement or statement of purpose but also identify and develop a business strategy. As a small-business owner, you are often not forced to do these steps and consequently skip over them. But this eliminates you from having a strategy which can create dysfunction.[1]

Amato's point to identify a plan of action in your business strategy is not one to ignore. As a retailer, your goal is to provide an end sale to a consumer. The question is: Aside from buying inventory, how do you do this?

Introducing and Managing Store Events

Upon arrival of inventory to your store, you should already have identified your plan of attack for how this product will affect your current inventory assortment, as well as how you plan to merchandise it, market it, and ultimately, sell it. Ideally, you are buying your product well in advance, allowing you to adequately plan for its arrival and all the layers of support that come with it. To get started, this includes creating a marketing calendar to help you promote your inventory and collective store at large.

Looking ahead no less than six months and even as far as one year, retailers can benefit from identifying their marketing plans via a dedicated store calendar. Used to enrich all the angles that affect your store's visibility—including social media, community events, customer-loyalty programs, and more—this calendar can help you to track, manage, and identify your in-store marketing goals.

Chicago-based retailer Angela Gianfrancesco shares her experience on planning ahead for her retail store:

> I work off a store calendar that I plan ahead by about nine months, and often it's even further planned out. Though old-fashioned, I have this calendar hanging on my backroom wall so that I am constantly reminded of it and, as a result, use it. There isn't a day that passes that I don't lean on this calendar as a reminder of what I need to do in order to stay on track with my sell-through goals. Essentially, this calendar identifies week by week what I have going on in my store, allowing me to visually see whether or not I have events planned or if I'm due for a merchandising window change. It also identifies any local events taking place, keeping my involvement with our community always top of my mind. Plus, I use different colors to reflect different things, such as red to identify that it's time for a new window display and blue to identify that we have an in-store event.[2]

For Gianfrancesco, making her calendar bold and big was critical to her attempt to actually use it. Prior to committing to a calendar, Gianfrancesco had leaned on memory alone to keep up with her store planning. She explains:

> Honestly, I was so busy that I never felt like I could stop to create a more organized way to keep up with inventory and store goals. It wasn't until I finally made the time that I realized it actually helps me and, ultimately, saves me time now as well.[3]

For some retailers, poster board–sized calendars won't do the trick. Fortunately, technology offers you many options that can seamlessly blend into your store operations. One technology to consider is SnapRetail's drag and drop calendar, which allows you to organize your month-by-month marketing plans in just minutes. You can add your own events and incorporate prewritten e-mail templates and social media posts from SnapRetail's library of options to make your marketing efforts quick yet effective. And, for retailers who prefer paper copies, you can simply print this calendar to reference as needed.

Creating a calendar is the easy step in this process compared with actually determining what needs to go on it. For merchants, identifying the best ways to attract customer attention and get them into your store always should be top of mind. This means that you should stage events and other promotions to help you achieve your goal.

RETAIL TIP

Using the SnapRetail calendar is one of the easiest ways to manage both your important in-store activities as well as your online marketing efforts. Not only can you plan ahead by scheduling your social posts and e-mails in advance, you can save time by using prewritten ideas from their social media library.

Below is an example of what SnapRetail's calendar looks like. Keep in mind that when visible online and in color, this calendar becomes clearer and easier to navigate.

Rich Kizer and Georganne Bender, internationally recognized retail keynote speakers and consultants, believe that consistent events are key:

> Every retailer needs to host two kinds of in-store events all year long: major and minor. In fact, you should host one major in-store event and two to three minor events each and every month. A major event is one that builds traffic and packs your store with customers. Do not confuse a major event with something that takes a long time to plan, however. A fashion show can be a major undertaking, but it's not a major event unless it attracts lots of potential customers who come to watch—and buy something while they're there. A minor event might be a Saturday full of "makits and takits," demonstrations, or miniclasses. Minor events draw customers to your store but should not take a lot of time to plan or implement. If the concept of events and promotions is new to you, then begin by running one major event and one minor event for each month of the year.[4]

Kizer and Bender's advice to plan both major and minor events into your store calendar should not be overlooked. Whether you sell pet supplies, craft items, women's fashions, or paint and hardware, there is a never-ending list of event possibilities for your niche store. One way to identify what types of events may be best suited for your customers is to ask them directly. Leaning on your social media networks as well as in-store staff communication, ask your customers point blank what types of events they'd love to see from you. Also, host a few events with a trial-and-error agenda that allows you to identify which are more successful than others.

RETAIL TIP

Geneva, Illinois-based retailer Shari Ralish opened her general merchandise store in February 2010. During the first year of business, Ralish rarely hosted in-store events and did not factor in the value that these could have on her business until 2012. At this time, she made monthly events a priority and routinely scheduled both mini and major events in her store, hosting on average six events a month. From 2011 to 2012, sales as a direct result of in-store events increased by 86 percent and from 2012 to 2013 sales increased by 27 percent due to store events. To continue this trend, Ralish looks ahead by no less than six months to ensure her event calendar is securely identified, ranging from vendor trunk shows to product sampling events to live music being played in her store. This also allows Ralish to communicate with her customers in a timely fashion, sharing everything that is taking place in her store.

When planning events, you should consider not only what the event is but also when it is. For example, you may find hosting the same event on a Wednesday night and a Sunday afternoon attracts more people one time versus the other. Don't let this bring you down, but instead attempt to understand why this may be. In response, begin to plan your future events accordingly. Only trial and error can help you to identify what's right for your customers and your store. The key here is to track each event so that you can lean on your event history to help increase your future event success. Some things to identify and track from each event include

1. *How far in advance did you plan the event?* If you add a last-minute event to your calendar and fail to give it a lot of marketing in advance, this could affect the event's success rate. Meanwhile, if you have an event identified six months out and strategically identify when you will announce it to your customers, prepare press releases for the local media, and incorporate details of the event into your e-mail marketing plans and social media, this will likely increase your chance for a stronger return on your event investment.

2. *How did you market each event?* For minor events, your marketing plan may be a combination of social media, in-store communication, and customer phone calls. However, for a major event, you may increase your marketing reach by doing postcard mailers to your store mailing list, reaching out to your local media for press attention, and working with outside vendors and like-minded businesses to reach a larger audience of potential customers and attendees. Always make sure to track and identify your marketing efforts—no matter how small or large—so that once the event is over, you can reflect back and see how these details affected your event. An easy way to do this is by creating an Excel spreadsheet that acts as a checklist of what you need to do and what you have already done. SnapRetail's online calendar also can support you in this tracking.

3. *Who was invited to each event?* Many retailers have open invitations and welcome anyone and everyone to their store events. This makes sense and is a great way to

increase your chance of stronger sales. However, there may be some exceptions to this rule, and on occasion, a dedicated invite list is ideal. One example of this would be if you are celebrating a store anniversary and want to reward your top customers with a special party, making it an invite-only event that you plan during traditionally closed hours. You could keep your store open until your normal closing time, welcoming all customers to enjoy your anniversary celebrations with product incentives, store specials, and other promotional experiences, and then close and lock your store for a private, invite-only celebration that begins after your store is officially closed to the public.

4. *What in-store experiences did you offer at each event?* Other than selling inventory and providing a place for your customers to shop, what did you do in your store that made your event more unique? Some ideas to consider would be having live music, offering an assortment of food and drinks, inviting a vendor to be on site and engage with customers, hosting a book signing, sharing product demonstrations, offering hands-on experiences that may include classes or making crafts, and offering customers minifacials, manicures, or other spa experiences. Depending on your niche audience, the ideas will vary, but the general idea to gain here is that by introducing experiences in your store that do not happen on a normal day, you are offering a stronger reason for consumers to want to attend your event. Remember to record the details of what it is you offer, allowing you to

reflect back on how this may have increased store sales and store traffic.

5. *What were both your expenses and sales as a direct result of each event?* The entire reason that events are undertaken is to make money, plain and simple. Naturally, there will be exceptions to this, such as if you host an event to raise awareness for a local charity, but for most of your events, making money will—and should be—your goal. Make sure that you set a sales goal for each event and plan your marketing efforts accordingly—helping you to reach your goals while also strengthening your chance of having a successful event. Be sure to also identify and track any additional expenses that you may incur when introducing events to your store, such as buying food, drinks, and other promotional items that could include balloons, paper plates, napkins, and more.

While creating, managing, and executing events may seem like a daunting task, the reward you see in sales should help you to stay motivated in keeping up with this agenda. Some final time-saving tips when preparing for in-store events come from Nolcha Events cofounder Kerry Bannigan:

You can never be too prepared when it comes to planning an event—no matter how large or small. Make an action plan, and consider the timing for your needs. Printing promotional materials, scheduling product deliveries, and buying refreshments for your event should all be considered well in advance to ensure that you don't miss a beat. It's also a good idea to consider preparing your store the evening prior to an event after it closes for the day, allowing you to get organized and ready to go without the chaos of customers or other store operational responsibilities. Finally, working with local businesses in your community to help promote your event can never hurt. Don't wait until the last minute to seek their support, however. Identify well in advance what local businesses you want to get involved in your event marketing, and then get in touch with them right away to identify how you can mutually support each other through this process.[5]

Highlighting Inventory Through Displays

Events certainly can help retailers to push sales and gain visibility, but your day-to-day existence will always play a key role in your retail success. Cathy Wagner, CEO and founder of RetailMAVENS, believes that the key to this is keeping things constantly moving around your store to increase the chance of sell-through:

> There are two things to consider when pushing inventory. You have to remain aware of the newer goods, but don't forget about the old stuff. Just because it's older does not mean that it needs to be marked down, although in cases where items aren't selling, this will be your solution. The key is to identify what is selling and what is not selling, no matter how new or old they are to your store assortment. One way to do this is to simply move things around your store to increase sell-through.[6]

Wagner's advice to move inventory around your store is a classic example of how merchandising can affect product sales. Agreeing with Wagner are retail experts Kizer and Bender, who believe that "your sales floor and displays require constant reinvention so that shoppers don't get bored and go somewhere else."[7]

RETAIL TIP

Lighting is commonly overlooked in retail spaces, however it has the potential to transform a store as well as a customer's experience within a retail environment. Proper lighting can entice customers to engage with products as well as lead them to certain areas of your store. On the contrary, dark spaces within retail environments may cause customers to strain their eyes or not view inventory on display at all.

Ensure your store has adequate lighting from all angles by incorporating accent lighting, high activity lighting (such as near your cash wrap or by a dressing room), ambient lighting that may include a singular store chandelier and case and shelve lighting to help highlight specific merchandise. While there is no single store formula for lighting, one general rule of thumb to follow is to change your lighting as you change your displays.

Keeping customers visually engaged in their shopping experience is a constant responsibility for retailers to keep up with. A great display may be just that—great—but after a while, it is no longer exciting, interesting, or engaging for your customers because it will inevitably become stale. Your job as a retailer is to never let this happen but instead consistently offer customers visually engaging experiences through constantly rotating store merchandise and displays.

Although every inch of your store must be kept up with regard to merchandising, some key areas to pay special attention to include

1. *Store windows.* A retailer's windows offer customers a first chance to form an impression of the store. And as the old saying goes, "First impressions have about three seconds to make a lasting impact." With this in mind, ask yourself if your store windows deliver a strong, lasting impression. If you've answered no, then it's critical that you add "change store window displays" to your immediate to-do list. Your goal should be to create a display that not only captures the attention of a previous customer but also entices a potential customer who has never been in your store. Windows offer the chance to highlight store inventory through displays but also are a great place to tell a story that represents your store versus actually highlighting what you sell. For example, you could create a window that has an oversized teddy bear sitting on a miniature chair with a bold, highlighted callout saying, "Let us take the weight off you this Valentine's Day," to demonstrate your store as the go-to spot for gift giving. Windows offer a chance to have fun and get creative, but ultimately, they must attract attention for you to attract sales. A good goal for keeping up with your window displays is to change them at least every two to three weeks.

2. *Immediate-right zone.* Studies tell us that time after time, customers turn to their right once they enter a store. Likely this is due to most folks being right-handed, but despite the reason, the real takeaway here is to focus on what you offer through display and merchandising to the immediate right in your store. Does this area capture customer attention? Are you highlighting must-have items here, or is this space wasted by not having a display at all? Consider what your store currently has in this area, and then plan to increase its merchandising value by strengthening your displays and product assortment there. Keep in mind that while you want your customers to stop, shop, and get engaged, this is also a high-traffic area for busy retailers, so you want to allow enough space for customer movement so that customers can easily pass each other as well.

3. *Store stoppers.* Sometimes recognized as store speed bumps, store stoppers are displays that stop customers in their tracks and get them focused on a display or product. Incorporating a few store stoppers throughout your retail space is key in keeping your customers engaged and shopping throughout their entire in-store experience. Rather than bundling your store-stopper displays close to each other, spread them out throughout your entire store to keep your customers moving and interested as they navigate your store space. Ideally, you should have about five store stoppers for every 500 square feet of store. They can be on tabletop displays or shelves but should allow customers to touch and interact with the product versus

making them have to ask for support in handling the featured items on display. Some stores may run into challenges here, such as high-end jewelry stores, but the idea still should be applied.

4. *Point-of-sale (POS) area.* There is no greater opportunity to increase your sales than by increasing each individual purchase being made. Retailers can apply this strategy to their stores simply by strengthening their POS areas with products that make great add-on sales or impulse buys for customers who have already decided to buy something. Essentially, this is your store's checkout spot, and when a customer lands here, it means that he or she has decided to make a purchase. This is your chance to increase the total purchase value by keeping the customer engaged with both interesting and necessity-based items that he or she can easily include in the purchase. Ideally, you want to keep the items merchandised in your POS area lower in price, relieving the customer of having to think too much about whether or not he or she should buy an item. Products priced at $1, $5, $10, and under $20 are great candidates for this area, keeping in mind that these prices should reflect your target audience and total store inventory assortment.

5. *Sale section.* Not all retailers have a dedicated sale section permanently in their stores, but whether you offer this seasonally or full time, this area offers a great chance to engage your customers through displays. Unlike your store-stopper sections and POS area, your sale section should lean more heavily on promoting the value of the

sale discount versus the product itself. If you are offering something at 50 percent off, for example, this message alone to customers will get them more excited than by highlighting what is actually for sale. Leaning on store signage companies such as BoutiqueVision.com for strong signage can help you achieve this.

In addition to these five key areas of store displays, you also should incorporate some merchandising techniques throughout your entire store to help increase sales. Among the best ways to do this is to cross-merchandise inventory, allowing multiple chances for your customers to see something on display. The main reason that this is so valuable for your business is that customers don't see everything in your store, so offering them the chance to see something in more than one spot increases the chance that they will actually experience it. Furthermore, repetition of products increases the consumer's impression of it, which also increases the chance that he or she will want to know more about a product and that ultimately increases your chance of selling that product.

Another tactic to apply to your store merchandising is that of staples and statements. If your store has items that are always in stock, such as plain white T-shirts or 8- by 10-inch frames, then create an area of your store that highlights your store staples. Train your customers through store signage and staff communication that you always have these staple items in stock, therefore helping to increase the chance that your store will become the go-to place for these identified items. On the contrary, if you have items that are seasonal, quick sellers, or trend items, these would fall into the statement category. These items deserve some highlighted attention as well and would merchandise well in your store-stopper spots and in window displays.

It's no secret that merchandising a store is a giant responsibility that requires not only skill but also time. To help make sure that you do not neglect this important store responsibility, add merchandising to your store calendar. Specifically, add what needs to be done, such as changing a front-window display or rearranging your POS display area. Generally speaking, you should rotate your in-store displays on a weekly basis to keep things fresh and exciting for your customers, and you should change your front-window displays no less than every two weeks.

Using Modern Technology in Your Store

In addition to classic merchandising techniques, retailers should consider how modern technology can be incorporated into their store strategy. iPads, for example, are being used increasingly for customer engagement. Some local retailers are introducing iPads into their stores as a way for customers to check in on their social media sites, such as on Facebook or FourSquare, in an effort to increase their store exposure through their customers' social networks. Others use iPads as a way to further communicate with their customers while they are on the sales floor.

"With an iPad in hand, it's easy to pull up your online store or an Instagram feed to show items as they might look in a customer's home or show customers other color options that might be momentarily out of stock,"[8] CEO Vaughan Rowsell of Vend, a loyalty and POS system company, shares with us.

RETAIL TIP

Modern technology will continue to impact retailers, however, some things will never change when it comes to creating a dynamic retail environment. For merchants, the sounds customers hear in their stores will always play a role in their selling success, retail experiences, and overall store environment. Fortunately, merchants can easily control their store space through sound by introducing customized radio stations to their stores.

California-based company, Retail Radio, provides licensed music and customized radio stations for independent retailers and other business owners. Their goal is to create a programmed music station that has the retailer's customer in mind in addition to creating commercials that promote each respective store. Essentially, Retail Radio creates in-store customer communication platforms through music and messaging. An added bonus is that the music they offer is all legally licensed, meeting all legal requirements for commercial businesses to use.

In addition to supporting retailers through customized music and messaging, Retail Radio provides other sensory-based support for merchants, addressing the needs of sight, sound, scent, and sales. You can learn more about Retail Radio at RetailRadio.biz.

As Vaughan explained, using an iPad as part of your store experience not only can help you as a merchant but also can keep customers engaged. Another added benefit that iPads offer retailers is the chance to eliminate a destination spot for checkout procedures and instead welcome any spot as a chance to ring up a sale. Rowsell continues:

The iPad as a POS is totally revolutionary for a number of reasons. The first, and possibly the most valuable, is that of its mobility. You can use an iPad anywhere, expanding your reach for potential customers and, ultimately, sales. Whether in food trucks, retail trucks, farmers' markets, at trade shows, or in your own store, your iPad can process transactions for your business. Because of this, what's so amazing for traditional brick-and-mortar retailers is that they can completely do away with the checkout counter and create a completely unique, customized retail experience. Imagine, an iPad POS system gives you the luxury to process sales anywhere while also eliminating the need for a checkout counter to disrupt your retail store design. Moreover, you do not have to interrupt the shopping experience as you drag your customers across the store to check stock levels or ring up their purchases. Instead, all of this can be taken care of right on your shop floor because of an iPad POS system.[9]

Certainly a portable POS system courtesy of an iPad has its benefits, as Rowsell points out. But one thing retailers should consider when introducing an iPad into their store's environment is its vulnerability to be damaged or possibly even stolen. If you do have a checkout area in your store, keeping your iPad in a designated spot within this location is one way to help manage its vulnerability. Also, you may even consider locking it in a drawer. However, the most effective way to keep your iPad accessible and useful is to have it securely fastened to an iPad stand that is locked in place within your store.

There are a number of models available for retailers to consider, but essentially retailers should look for an iPad stand that securely locks their iPad in place, only releasing it on key retrieval or by entering a code. Retailers who want a portable iPad that can move around the store with them should consider iPad carts and other moving devices that allow retailers to easily bring along iPads anywhere in the store while keeping their hands free to support their customers and attend to other store responsibilities. These types of iPad cases, carts, and other security-focused products may be available from your POS provider but are also available at iPadEnclosures.com.

Identifying Whether Mobile Commerce Matters

iPads are certainly a technology of the present and future that we don't foresee leaving the retail scene for a long, long time. That said, mobile technology continues to be a popular conversation in retail, but it should be recognized that m-commerce is not growing as originally anticipated among small-business owners. *M-commerce*, otherwise known as *selling via mobile devices*, represents a minority among Internet-based purchases, and most consumers still lean on their computers or tablets when buying online.

Jason Richelson, founder and CEO of ShopKeep POS, has spent his entire career in retail and believes that similar to credit-card adoption, not all small businesses will embrace mobile technology:

The big talking point within the payments world in 2013 has really been mobile. But I have to say, I've seen little to none of that talk translate for small businesses. There are many predictions about 2014 as the year of mobile, but I don't think small retailers by and large will move that quickly. Take credit-card adoption, for example. Despite more than 40 years of use, a large percentage of small businesses still don't accept them. Similarly, the adoption curve for mobile payments will not shift significantly overnight. There needs to be incentive, it needs to be easy, and there needs to be demand from consumers.[10]

With consumers in mind, a retailer's greater interest in mobile technology should be in embracing the idea that customers likely will engage with their phones while in his or her store, although this doesn't always mean that customers are competitive shopping online. Often customers refer to their phones simply to call family and friends for product advice, send pictures to friends for feedback, seek coupons for the immediate store they are in, or search for product reviews of a particular item. Competitive shopping does exist via mobile phones, but this reality isn't one to sweat over if your in-store experience is delivering strong engagement, displays, and marketing—thereby giving your customers an experience they simply cannot get online.

Finally, never lose sight of the fact that shopping truly is a sport for many consumers. Just as in a competitive game of basketball, football, or any other sport, shopping offers the chance for you to win or lose when it comes to attracting and keeping customer attention. Every detail that affects your business must constantly be nurtured and attended to, just like every detail of any professional sport matters. In the end, it's only those who are willing to work their hardest despite obstacles and setbacks who will remain standing and ultimately become winners in the competitive game of retail.

* * *

Hopefully by now you have realized just how much range and time are necessary to manage and market a retail store. In the chapters that follow, we'll unveil ways to apply press and marketing to your retail business as ways to generate some well-deserved attention to the hard work you have done to create your unique store.

Action Guide

Research shows that customers prefer store layouts that allow for easy navigation and movement throughout their shopping experience. Moreover, research tells us that customers respond, react, and ultimately make purchasing decisions based on all their senses— not just that of sight alone.

To help you maximize your customers' experience in your store, consider each of the five senses and take action to improve their role in your store:

1. *Sight.* From the exterior of your store to the entire interior store space, identify whether your store is attractive and captivating in gaining customer attention. Next,

look for any debris, dirt, or dust throughout your entire store space that needs to be cleaned up. Then visually identify whether a stroller, wheelchair, cane, or other assistive device would be able to be used comfortably in your store. These visual observations are ones that many customers identify when forming an impression of your store and should be improved if they do not currently cater to consumers' needs and ideals.

2. *Touch.* Instinctively, customers want to touch things and experience products hands-on. Walk through your current store space and identify whether you offer a space that encourages customers to touch and interact with your inventory. Keeping products at eye level for hands-on engagement is a good way to make customers feel welcome to touch your products. Incorporating signage as necessary that states "Feel free to sample" or "Please do not touch this display, but we hope you will touch our other ones" can lend a helping hand in encouraging your customers to touch and interact with your store products as appropriate. For those of you who have customers who bring their children with them, create a dedicated area or simply have a small basket with toys or washable crayons and paper to distract kids from touching your inventory and to free up the attention of your customer.

3. *Sound.* Identify what your store currently sounds like. Is it the sound of blaring music or coworkers chatting about their weekend plans? Possibly it sounds silent, with only the occasional buzz of a door opening and closing. Customers tend to stay in environments that make them

feel comfortable, and sound plays a big role in this. Make it a rule for employees to eliminate personal phone calls, store gossip, or any other unnecessary conversations that customers may overhear. In addition, choose music that is neutrally accommodating to your diverse range of customers. Keep the sound level of your music at a moderate level as well that does not make customers uncomfortable and still allows them to hear you speak and allows them to speak to each other.

4. *Smell.* Aroma can be good or bad. What does your store smell like? Identify what your store smells like and whether or not this affects your customers' experiences. It's possible that a local bakery's aroma trickles into your store, and thus you gain a scent out of your control. Or maybe you choose to burn incense that some customers find unattractive in scent. Whatever your current situation is, strive to identify a single scent that you can always apply to your store and that customers will associate with your store as time passes. Scents such as chocolate, vanilla, coffee, and pine are often perceived as mass-appealing scents, whereas the scents of flowers or certain spices are not as preferred by the masses. Pick a store scent for your store that is subtle yet complementing to your retail space, and then make this your signature scent for customers to associate with your store.

5. *Taste.* Even if your store does not sell food or offer an opportunity to cater to your customers' taste buds, you can still engage your audience through the power of taste. Choose a signature sweet, such as bite-sized choco-

lates or peppermints, and always have these available for your customers to take. A small glass of water can even provoke taste buds and may extend your support in delivering strong customer care. If your store has not introduced taste to its strategy of supporting customers, it's time to do so.

8

Applying Press and Marketing to Your Business

Lack of attention, not lack of time, is the problem.
We all have twenty-four-hour days.

—*Zig Ziglar (1926–2012), author and motivational speaker*

RETAILERS TODAY are bombarded with places to go, things to do, and customers to serve. Despite their busy schedules, however, customers have high expectations from retailers and expect their consumer experiences to be top-notch. Also, customers have choices when it comes to making their buying decisions, which makes any retailer's attempt to stand out in his or her local marketplace that much more important.

Long-time independent retailer Cynthia Sutton, owner of The Silver Barn in Columbus, Texas, believes that despite busy schedules and big-box competition, locally-based merchants have some key advantages that larger retailers do not. Sutton explains:

> Local, independent retailers can react to community needs instantly. For example, here in our small town there was a horrible car accident where a young child was seriously injured and a grandmother killed. The car that hit them had no insurance. We sprang into action and started a fundraiser with other local merchants. Our local Walmart, however, could not participate because they had to wait to get corporate approval.[1]

This type of quick response is just one example of how local merchants can support their communities and local customers, as well as generate awareness for their stores. In addition to reacting to a worthy cause, this also provides a great reason to gain publicity for a store. Unlike some marketing efforts, publicity does not cost you a lot of money—if any—yet you can gain exposure to both existing and potential customers. Exposure through publicity adds value to a merchant and often makes a store more memorable. The key here, however, is having a story to tell that the press would be interested in highlighting among their media outlets. Fortunately, this goes hand in hand with also creating a store environment that encourages customers to come back.

"We can't compete with volume pricing, mass advertising, and depth of inventory. However, we can deliver stronger customer service and more unique inventory than big-box stores. This is extremely valuable to consumers,"[2] explains Sutton.

HOW TO WRITE A PRESS RELEASE

Publicity, when managed internally, costs you nearly nothing except time and possibly a few additional dollars. For the most part, however, press is free. With this in mind, understanding how to write a press release can help you pitch your store to local and national media, increasing store visibility and encourage a growth in sales. Using the tips below, learn more about how to write a press release.

1. A press release is a statement intended to share noteworthy news, event details, and other interesting facts with the media. When writing a press release, you want to keep the audience in mind and answer the questions "who", "what", "when", "where" and "why".

2. All critical information should be concisely summarized within the first paragraph of your press release, allowing busy editors and other members of the media to quickly identify what it is you want to share. The following paragraphs should elaborate on the details shared. Including quotes from relevant people involved in the news you are sharing, whether yourself or a store vendor, for example, can add value to the press release.

3. Press releases should ideally be no more than one page and should be constructed in standard press release format. This includes identifying your store name, contact person, and contact details in the top left corner, providing a captivating title and supporting tagline for your press release and providing the release date and city of the press release prior

to your first sentence. In addition, the paragraphs that follow should share detailed information about your store and the purpose of your press release while offering general or interesting facts. An example would be:

Ma's General Store
Contact: Jane Smith
Phone: 555.555.5555
Email: shop@masgeneralstore.com

Ma's General Store Introduces Extended Shopping Hours
on Weekends
Doors to Open at 9 am to Accommodate Customer Requests

May 1, 2014 (Geneva, IL)—Kicking off the spring shopping season, Ma's General Store is excited to welcome customers at 9 am every Saturday and Sunday into their downtown Geneva store. After years of customers requesting earlier shopping hours, Ma's General Store looks forward to supporting customers on their weekends shopping for general household supplies and other everyday necessities. And, all customers who shop Ma's General Store before 11 am will be offered complimentary coffee or juice.

"It's important for us to keep our customers happy and these additional store hours will allow them to get their weekend errands off to an early start, which we're thrilled to support," store owner Jane Smith states.

Based in downtown Geneva in the historic shopping district, Ma's General Store is a favorite destination among local residents to stock up on household supplies and everyday necessities. In addition to their well-stocked shelves, Ma's General Store will be offering their early bird customers complimentary coffee and juice.

To learn more about Ma's General Store, to speak with owner Jane Smith, or to request high-resolution images, please contact us 555.555.5555 or shop@masgeneralstore.com.

# # #

4. Press releases should aim to be concise, clear, correct, and courteous, keeping your audience's attention while being direct and informative in the news you share. At the end of your release, identify its conclusion with three number signs. This indicates it is complete and is part of the general format of writing a press release.

5. Sending a press release does not guarantee press will be received. Be sure to follow up with your media contacts and respect their outreach to you, as well, should they want more information. Like you, media professionals are busy people so try and get back to them as soon as possible should they want more information about the news you shared.

Customer service and unique inventory are two well-known factors that make independent retailers stand out from big-box stores. Yet merchants often underestimate their value in the press.

As Sutton believes, "Basic is great at big box; special is great at independents." With this in mind, I encourage you to constantly seek out what makes your store stand out among others. Is it the unique story of an employee of your store who happens to excel at customer service? Is it the one-of-a-kind products by local artisans that you sell made? Is it the fact that your store, unlike so many others, offers an experience that can't be duplicated anywhere else? Or possibly, is it a random customer experience you had that offers a great story to share with the press?

As a retailer, you need not only to strive to make your store memorable and unique but also recognize when unique and memorable things happen within your store environment. In response to these scenarios, you should be prepared to share the details with customers via the press, the Internet, through e-mail, and via other avenues that can generate awareness of your store.

Suzy Teele, COO of SnapRetail.com, a ready-to-use marketing solution for independent retailers, believes that while customer service and product assortment add value to a shopping experience, merchants today should not ignore the value of their store personality as well. She explains:

"I think the biggest misconception that retailers face today is that sometimes they rely too much on their products to get customers into their stores. Brands go in and out of favor, so brands alone aren't enough. Independent retailers should remember that it's not only the merchandise; it's also

RETAIL TIP

Online marketing and press can help generate store visibility, but don't neglect the power of good old-fashioned store packaging. A famous example of this is the Tiffany blue box or bag, recognized by customers as a purchase of luxury and beauty. While your store may not cater to the same clientele that Tiffany does, this should not keep you from aiming to have strong store packaging.

An easy way to enhance your store packaging is to invest in a signature bag that is used any time a customer makes a purchase. Rather than use a generic brown or other colored bag that has no brand impressions on it, consider creating a customized bag that current and future customers can begin to recognize you by. Over time, your bag will become a recognized symbol for your store, increasing customer awareness of your business.

Additional tips to help brand your store through packaging include using the same tissue paper, ribbon, and gift wrapping paper every time they are needed. In other words, consistency is key here. To help you accomplish this, lean on an outside company that specializes in supporting businesses such as independent retailers through packaging. One such company is Premier Packaging, a small business themselves who support retailers through sales of gift boxes, gift bags, tissue paper, ribbons and customized options to help strengthen a retailer's brand and visibility.

how they merchandise the merchandise. In other words, creating a strong store personality and stories around the merchandise will drive store traffic and reduce the focus on competitive pricing.[3]

Teele's perspective is common among retail experts and supporters, with the idea that product alone cannot make you a successful retailer. She continues:

In my experience, the stores that I have seen succeed have been able to do so because they make their customers feel as though they are part of something special. They make customers *want* to shop there. This is accomplished by creating that strong store personality, sharing that personality through social media, and inviting customers to be part of it through e-mail marketing and other promotional events. Using the latest marketing tools, independent retailers can create their brands and store personalities, positioning them to effectively compete with big-box retailers.[4]

Companies that provide marketing tools for independent retailers are becoming more and more common. SnapRetail is a great example of this type of company, providing ready-to-use marketing for independent retailers in a variety of ways. Founded in 2010, SnapRetail provides prewritten content in the form of e-mails, social media posts, event marketing, and more, all specific to independent retailers. Their easy-to-use marketing solution helps retailers to better manage their time while becoming more engaged in all the necessary avenues of retail, including marketing, social media, e-mail, event planning, and general promotional exposure. Teele says:

> SnapRetail customers often see about a 15 to 20 percent increase in sales and a stronger engagement through social media with continual use of our solution. Our most successful retailers engage with their customers on social media sites like Facebook at least once a day and send meaningful e-mails two to three times per week.[5]

In Chapter 9, we'll further discuss how SnapRetail's marketing solutions specifically apply to online efforts.

Using E-mail to Communicate Store Messages

Increasing your e-mail open rate, which identifies how many people who receive your e-mails actually read them, is an important goal to have. Yet, retailers often struggle with what to say and how to create a strong layout for their e-mails. SnapRetail's library of prewritten and professionally designed e-mail templates does the work for you, even offering a calendar feature with the software so that you can schedule and manage your e-mail and other marketing communications. Incorporating solutions such as this into your marketing plan is a great way to make your to-do list easier without compromising the success of your store. In fact, the goal is to increase it.

Marketing communications manager Jessica Moretti of Snap-Retail is always searching for the best messages retailers can share with their customers, providing with us five tips that retailers should lean on when creating e-mails for their customers:

1. *Content, content, content!* Content is key to engaging e-mail marketing. Always ensure that your e-mails contain content that is timely, relevant, and valuable to your readers.

2. *Lights, camera, action!* A good e-mail contains one clear call to action (CTA). Your readers should know exactly what you want them to do, and it should be relatively easy for them to complete the action—"Shop our sale," "Visit our website," "Pin your favorite product."

3. *Keep it simple, stupid (KISS)!* Borrow a page from the Navy's handbook and follow the KISS rule when it comes to e-mail design. Keep it simple by using a color palette of no more than three complementary colors, easy-to-read fonts, and a structured format.

4. *First impressions are everything.* Give your subject line the love and attention it deserves. It's the first thing your readers will see and can make or break whether your readers will open your e-mail.

5. *Gone in less than 60 seconds.* Research shows that you have less than 60 seconds to grab your readers' attention before they click away from your e-mail. Because of this, it is imperative that your headlines and calls to actions are more compelling than that video of a sneezing panda your reader just received from a friend.[6]

Keeping these five tips in mind, remember to also consider how often you reach out to your customers via e-mail. You don't want to bombard your customers' e-mail in-boxes every day, but you don't want to go too long in between e-mails either. Recently, Retail Minded surveyed its retail audience and asked them how often they prefer to receive e-mails from companies they choose to follow, as well as how often they send out e-mails to their own e-mail marketing lists. In response to both questions, retailers surveyed through RetailMinded.com, and its social media networks identified once a week for each scenario. Although there will be exceptions, if you have something worth sharing with your audience on a weekly basis, an e-mail blast scheduled once a week is a good starting point to plan for your own e-mail marketing efforts.

To further support your e-mail outreach, you want to also evaluate the success of each e-mail blast you send out. Analyzing the results of each e-mail campaign allows you to understand what is most effective in your e-mail efforts. E-mail marketing providers such as SnapRetail, Constant Contact, and Mail Chimp all offer e-mail analysis as part of their services, and we encourage you to make it a priority to evaluate these results on a consistent basis.

Among the many things an e-mail report may tell you is which e-mails were opened the most (their open rates), what days and times e-mails sent were most read, and whether or not promotions or incentives offered via e-mail gained a stronger return than other e-mails sent. A little studying of these reports can go a long way, so be sure to add this to your retail to-do list.

Using the Internet as a Marketing Platform

E-mail marketing is nearly a classic technique compared with other online marketing efforts, yet it shouldn't be ignored as you incorporate additional Internet-based marketing into your sales and marketing strategy. One company that aims to specifically support independent merchants in doing this is Boutique Window. This Nebraska-based company developed software to help retailers show off their latest inventory, new arrivals, store promotions, and more via a merchant's own website and social media. With a setup that takes only minutes, retailers can upload and edit photos of their store merchandise, add product details to support their images, and publish immediately on Facebook, Twitter, Pinterest, and their individual business websites. Doing this helps retailers to keep their stores top of mind for their customers' shopping lists, an important factor to include in your own retail marketing.

Cofounder of Boutique Window, Courtney Rodgers, believes that even if you don't sell online, your online visibility is something you can't ignore:

> Connecting with shoppers online is essential to the success of your business, even if you don't actually have an online store. Shoppers today are engrossed in the digital world, making your store visibility possible with only a few simple clicks. With the rapid growth of social networks and improvements in local search options, customers can access any information they want online with just a click or two. Of course, if you aren't online, then your store will miss out on these opportunities. Even brick-and-mortar stores with

no plans to sell online should still have an online presence for this reason alone.[7]

Being top of mind is ideal for any retailer, but those who have yet to make an online presence are bound to be left out in the cold. Being visible online is a must these days, even if you have no plans to ever sell via the web. Creating a website that complements your in-store experience and brand identity is key, allowing customers to understand your store personality both online and offline more cohesively.

In 2012, e-commerce sales generated $231 billion in the United States alone, according to market research firm Forrester. This company also found that the growth of e-commerce, which in 2012 accounted for about 8 percent of total retail sales in the United States, is expected to outperform the growth of brick-and-mortar stores over the next five years, reaching $370 billion by 2017. With these types of numbers, independent retailers should not challenge the question of *if* they want to sell online but rather *when* they will start. Fortunately, creating an online presence is easy thanks to e-commerce templates from a variety of providers. Leading this market is Shopify.com, an online company that supports emerging or existing retailers and wholesalers in their efforts to create savvy, customer-friendly online shops. Shopify's 24/7 support and easy-to-customize website templates are ideal for independent merchants looking to get online quickly, effectively, and affordably. In Chapter 9, we'll discuss how you can maximize your online success in more detail, specifically looking at social media and e-commerce.

"Indie merchants have a variety of challenges, but their ultimate challenge is always getting enough traffic in their stores—either physical or online—to keep their lights on,"[8] Texan retailer Sutton states. While this could not be truer, it's often the retailers themselves who lead themselves to turned-off lights. To avoid this becoming a reality for your store, choose to be aggressive in your store marketing efforts to keep up with your competition and your customers alike.

Finally, to help you further navigate your marketing success as an independent merchant, we've identified a list of must-know businesses to help you reach your marketing goals. We also encourage you to explore Appendix A for a more comprehensive list of businesses and resources that can help your business reach its full potential.

Resources Every Independent Retailer Should Know About

1. *American Independent Business Alliance: www.amiba.net* This is a nonprofit organization that helps communities and retailers launch and operate buy-local campaigns to support local entrepreneurs and economies.
2. *Boutique Window: www.boutiquewindow.com* This company provides online marketing to showcase inventory via your website or social media outlets, allowing retailers to engage their customers with new-product arrivals and more.

3. *MOO: www.moo.com* This company provides business cards, postcards, store hangtags, and other print goods that are stylish in design and easy to customize to your unique store needs.

4. *Premier Packaging: www.retailpackaging.com* This company provides packaging solutions that cater to retailers looking to incorporate packaging options such as bags, gift boxes, and tissue paper as part of their store identity and marketing.

5. *Retail Radio: www.retailradio.biz* Customize your in-store experience with music that is catered uniquely to your store and your customer while also incorporating customized messaging to create the best possible ambiance for your unique retail space.

6. *Shopify: www.shopify.com* This company provides easy-to-customize online store templates that help you to sell online efficiently, affordably, and professionally.

7. *Smart Sign: www.smartsign.com* Signage can support your store communication to help customers navigate your store space and maximize their store experience. Use for display, merchandising, or promotion and incorporate safety signage such as "Emergency Exit" or "Employees Only" as well.

8. *SnapRetail: www.snapretail.com* This company provides prewritten content and general marketing support that includes e-mail, social media, and event management specific to independent retailers.

9. *Tripar International: www.tripar.com* This company provides visual displays and fixtures that help you to beauti-

fully showcase product, engage customers, and drive sales with products that include tabletop displays, jewelry stands, easels, point-of-sale (POS) accessories and more.

10. *Vend: www.vendhq.com.* Manage your customer loyalty, inventory, and POS systems with one, easy-to-use software program that is accessible on an iPad, computer, smartphone, or any device with a web browser. While not marketing-specific, this company's POS software can help you streamline the entire operational procedures of your store, including customer management and exposure.

* * *

Using this chapter as your reference, you can see just how many businesses are available to help you reach your full marketing potential, as well as the need to increase your store's visibility. In the chapters ahead, we'll discuss additional ways to generate more exposure for your store, ultimately, to help increase sales.

Action Guide

Creating a store personality is a key step in separating your business from others. Merchants should take the time to identify how they want to be perceived not only by customers but also by their competition. Identifying the characteristics of your store is an important step, although it's also critical to recognize whether your store's perception matches your intended reality. One way to do this is to put yourself in the shoes of a customer.

Putting your emotions aside, challenge yourself to take on the role of customer in your store. Be quick to judge and impatient as you evaluate your store, allowing yourself to hold characteristics of common customers in today's busy marketplace. With your mindset committed to being that of a customer instead of a store owner, walk into your store and critique your store's environment. Answer the following questions as objectively as possible. Moreover, invite at least three and ideally up to 10 other people to complete this same exercise.

1. What do you immediately view as most appealing in the store? Why?
2. What do you immediately identify as least appealing in the store? Why?
3. What did it feel like when you first entered the store? Explain your emotional reaction, such as "welcoming," "claustrophobic," "engaging," "distracting," or anything else you may feel.
4. Are there any distractions in the retail space that take you away from shopping or wanting to browse the store? This may include people, noise, displays, or anything else.
5. What items, if any, look out of place in the store? Why do you think this is?
6. What items stand out the most? Why?
7. Do any items strike you as being out of place within the store assortment? Please explain.
8. Are there any items that you don't see in the store assortment but believe would make sense to have? Please explain.

9. Do the displays engage you as a customer? How so?

10. What areas of the store appear most accommodating for shopping and enjoying? Please explain why you think this.

11. Which areas of the store do not attract you to them at all? Please explain why you think this may be.

12. Does the store appear clean to you? Do you see any visible dust or other dirt?

13. For stores with public restrooms, what impression does the restroom give off to a customer observing it?

14. Does the cash-wrap area provide customers with a place to rest their purse or sign a receipt and enjoy their checkout experience?

15. Do the walls need a fresh coat of paint?

16. Are there visible areas of the store that look as if they need some TLC or some kind of repair? Please explain.

17. Do any store fixtures overpower the inventory or restrict you as a customer from shopping and enjoying the store experience?

18. Does the store signage attract your attention? Why or why not? Is it easy to identify what is on sale, store policies, special announcements, and more?

19. Does any unstocked inventory appear to be on the selling floor?

20. What is your ultimate, final impression of the store?

Once completed, review your responses with an open mind, and identify common responses among all participants. Work to strengthen the areas identified as needing help, positioning yourself to better support your customers and your overall business success.

PART III

Making a Mark in the Economy

9

Making Your Presence Online

Make your product easier to buy than your competition,
or you will find your customers buying from them, not you.

—Mark Cuban (1958–present), Dallas Mavericks owner,
businessman, investor

O NE OF the greatest misconceptions about brick-and-mortar
independent retail is that it's a solitary endeavor. Small-business
owners have countless options beyond their store walls, allowing
them to connect and engage with vendors, retail supporters, and customers alike. Among these options are e-commerce and social media.

E-commerce has gained a bad reputation among independent
retailers because of the success of big-box players such as Amazon,
Walmart, Staples, and others. Although this is understandable, it
doesn't mean that e-commerce should be ignored by independent
retailers. In fact, it means that it should be embraced. Choosing

not to engage in e-commerce only eliminates the additional revenue and exposure that e-commerce can provide. *Internet Retailer Magazine*'s editor in chief Don Davis shared his thoughts on the value of selling online, emphasizing a retailer's total reach of potential consumers:

> Small brick-and-mortar retailers can reach a much broader audience online than they can in their physical storefronts alone. With a physical store, you can only reach the consumers within driving distance; with an online store, you can at least reach across the country and, with a little effort, the world. Most consumers are shopping online, and a big majority of affluent consumers with the most disposable income are included in this audience. Without an e-commerce site, an independent retailer can't reach millions of consumers.[1]

Harley Finkelstein, an entrepreneur, attorney, and chief platform officer at Shopify.com, agrees with Davis, sharing his belief that merchants should not differentiate between offline or online sales but instead look at them together. "In my opinion, the future of e-commerce belongs to small businesses. This is the biggest opportunity for retailers since farmer's markets began hundreds of years ago,"[2] Finkelstein explains.

Embracing E-commerce

Expanding your reach among potential customers seems like a no-brainer, but many retailers are still hesitant to introduce an online business as a supplement to their brick-and-mortar stores. Fortunately, the hassles and frustrations that previously existed with managing online shops are a thing of the past thanks to companies such as Shopify.com, an online company committed to helping small businesses create beautiful e-commerce stores through its easy-to-implement website templates. Founded in 2006, Shopify has grown to support over tens of thousands of online retailers across the world. Through its platform, users can easily and quickly create their own online shops without having to deal with all the technical work involved in developing a customized website. Essentially, Shopify eliminates the hassle of running an online store—something busy store owners can appreciate—yet delivers an opportunity for brick-and-mortar merchants to expand their sales and visibility online.

"People sometimes have this perception that setting up an online store is difficult and expensive, but that's not the case,"[3] Finkelstein explains. In addition to Finkelstein's own two cents, we have experienced using a Shopify-based e-commerce site firsthand on more than one occasion. Having been able not only to build a website through Shopify but also to navigate and shop Shopify-managed websites as a consumer, our collective experience allows us to confidently support Shopify.com as our number one choice for e-commerce-based website template options. Among the variety of reasons we prefer Shopify is that the company offers a diverse range of options that cater to all types of retailers while making the user experience from both the retailers' and the consumers' perspectives easy and—dare we say it—enjoyable.

For example, Shopify offers a number of e-commerce packages that fit any retailer's budget. With options that include attractive website templates, product images, gift cards, shopping-cart features, carrier shipping, and much more, retailers can confidently manage an online store without wondering if they have covered all their bases. Another perk of using an e-commerce template company such as Shopify is that as your business grows and your online sales increase, you can comfortably expand your e-commerce support via Shopify with just a few simple clicks. One example of a retailer that did just that is Beardbrand, whose website is Beardbrand.com.

Beardbrand, a modern retailer that sells grooming kits, beard care, and other lifestyle products for men, first created a Shopify-based store in early 2013. Founder Eric Bandholz had been blogging about beards for a while, so he knew a few things about being visible online. This said, he didn't know everything he needed to start and manage an e-commerce business. This is where Shopify .com entered the picture. Despite having only three products and no established sales, Beardbrand found instant success and was even featured in the *New York Times*—an impressive accomplishment for a retailer that only a year prior had no e-commerce business. Since then, Beardbrand.com has expanded its line and now generates up to $60,000 monthly—a number that continues to increase.

Another online success story from a very different niche retail market is that of Fringe Sport, a Texas-based retailer that caters to the at-home gym enthusiast. Brothers Peter and Alex Keller founded Fringe Sport in 2010, and within the first year, the company brought in $100,000 through its online Shopify-based store. By 2012, the Keller brothers had introduced additional brick-and-mortar locations as well as a wholesale program, collectively generating $1 million in revenue in 2012 alone. In 2013, that number grew to $3 million. Of that $3 million, 60 percent came from the online store.

RETAIL TIP

One of the many perks of using a template-based e-commerce website is that it makes website management easy and accessible for merchants to use. An example of this can be found below in a screen shot from Shopify.com, where you can easily identify when orders were received online and how much each order was for. In addition to identifying daily summaries of online sales, Shopify.com identifies weekly, monthly, and total sales made throughout each year. Collectively, their extensive reporting and e-commerce management help retailers identify sales trends, missed opportunities, and more.

Having a niche market certainly helps retailers Beardbrand and Fringe Sport stand out in the marketplace, but another key factor to recognize here is the design and aesthetics of their online stores. Both stores are easy to navigate, allowing customers from any part of the world to shop their web-based stores with ease. Supporting your customers with a well-thought-out, easy-to-navigate website is no different than supporting your customers with a well-thought-out, easy-to-navigate physical storefront. Both are critical in keeping your customers' attention, but they vary tremendously in the tricks and tips necessary to accomplish this goal. Unlike running your own brick-and-mortar store, managing an e-commerce shop doesn't take as much time to set up, manage, or merchandise— allowing you to nearly effortlessly introduce this to your sales strategy, particularly if you already have an existing brick-and-mortar store with stock ready to sell. The key here, as already mentioned, is using a template-based e-commerce website such as Shopify.com versus taking the time to create your own web store from scratch. Not only will this save you time, but you will also likely save money when positioning yourself online in this way.

Whether you currently have an online store, plan to introduce your first one soon, or are still up in the air as to whether or not you want to bring your business online, the following 10 tips should be considered when building your web presence:

1. *Focus on what's unique to you.* As *Internet Retailer Magazine*'s editor in chief Don Davis shares: "There is no point in trying to compete in selling standard paper towels or socks with Amazon.com or Walmart.com. They'll kill you in price. Instead, focus on something

EXPERT SPOTLIGHT

According to Boutique Window cofounder, Courtney Rodgers, having an online presence as a retailer is no longer optional.

"Doing a poor job of representing your store online reflects negatively on your store's brand. Keeping your website and social media profiles up to date should be worked into your regular business schedule. Make sure you're posting new merchandise to your website as it arrives and stick to a consistent social media schedule as well."[4]

Rodger's advice to make your online presence a priority isn't shared by her opinion alone.

"Forrester Research estimates that in 2014, 50.5% of in-store retail sales will be influenced by online research. Communicating what is currently in your store is the best way to attract new customers and turn existing customers into repeat, loyal shoppers. Being online will help you do this,"[5] Rodgers explains.

more unusual, such as a selection of crocheting wool, local handcrafted items, or a deep selection of olive oil to capture a buying market for your goods online."[6]

2. *Create strong product descriptions.* Unlike a physical storefront that has a salesperson available to answer customer questions or share product information, an online store needs to speak for itself. Make sure that your online written communication is detailed and easy to understand, allowing your online customers to gain as much information about your products as possible. Furthermore, you should aim to provide engaging information to complement the

great product details you are sharing. Keeping your audience intrigued will affect your customer engagement, so choosing the right words is critical when selling on the web.

3. *Use crisp, clear images of the products you sell online.* While your product descriptions need to be strong, you do not want to neglect your product pictures either. Without customers being able to touch, hold, smell, taste, or otherwise engage with the products they are interested in, your product images must really stand out and capture your customers' attention. Depending on the product you are selling, multiple images per product may be necessary to really allow your customers to feel as if they have a solid understanding of what that product truly looks like. If taking pictures is not your expertise, be sure to request product images from your vendors, and also consider an outside company such as BuyersPacket.com, which offers a studio effect service that can take any picture and make it appear to have been professionally photographed. You also should aim to have high-resolution images on your website as well.

4. *Be consistent in your product layout.* With both your product descriptions and images to be considered here, you want to have a consistent layout for your entire online inventory. In other words, do not give expanded details on one item and write a brief overview on another or show a crisp, clear picture of one product and then a blurry, low-resolution image of another. Customers want their entire online shopping experience to be great—not just some of it. Consistency is key in achieving this.

5. *Identify your shopping cart option at all times.* When selling online, a shopping cart is referred to as the place in which products land once a customer identifies them as something they would like to purchase. Having this shopping cart visible with an icon allows your customers to check items in their carts and easily check out when they are ready. Complicating these two critical steps by making your customers search for this part of your website will only decrease your chance of capturing their sales.

6. *Display company contact information, an about us page, and other highlighted details.* By now, hopefully, you've realized that an easy-to-see and easy-to-navigate website is key to successfully selling online. This also holds true for any other details a customer may want to gain from your website, including company contact details, deals and promotions, an about us page, and more. While sharing these details may not seem like a big deal, what you are really doing here is gaining trust from your customer. Consumers online want to feel secure when shopping, and offering them easy-to-access details about your company can help you achieve this.

7. *Offer multiple payment options.* The last thing an online merchant wants to see happen is getting a bunch of shopping carts filled to purchase only to have them become abandoned. Among the reasons this may happen is because a customer does not like the payment options available online. When identifying what choices you want your customers to have in making an online purchase, variety is key. Having multiple payment options

ensures that you meet multiple customer preferences, saving you yet another hassle of trying to identify what is best. Including PayPal and multiple credit card options is typically most preferred by customers.

8. *Lean on e-commerce specific resources to help you manage your business.* The annual Internet Retailer Conference and Exhibition (IRCE) offers 200+ speakers over a four-day period, attracting 600 or more e-commerce technology and service vendors together in one place. As Davis tells us, "Whatever you need to sell online, you can learn about it and find the right providers for your goals at IRCE."[7] This is a great event to consider attending, although you also can stay in the comfort of your store and visit InternetRetailer.com for free, trusted e-commerce support as well as refer to Shopify.com's Ecommerce University and globally recognized blog for additional e-commerce news, education, and support as well.

9. *Avoid charging for shipping whenever possible.* We certainly understand that this is not always the case, but if you can factor in occasional free shipping opportunities or eliminate shipping costs altogether, you will be more likely to increase your online sales. One way to incorporate this into your sales strategy is to eliminate offering product discounts, such as 15 percent off, and instead apply these savings to your shipping. Customers nowadays are becoming increasingly more dependent on free shipping, thanks to our big-box competitors, so you want to acknowledge this reality head on rather than avoid it.

When shipping costs are necessary, make sure that you offer the most economical options possible.

10. *Keep your customers top of mind in every decision you make.* Are you trying to attract Generation Y consumers or near-retirement folks? Whomever your audience, never lose sight of them as you as develop your online store. If your preferred customers are more Generation Y than baby boomers, consider introducing videos on your website. Be proactive in knowing who your customers are and catering to their unique online preferences, therefore better supporting their shopping experiences. This really isn't that much different from choosing to create one display in your physical store versus another, developing it with a unique audience in mind. And true to every decision you make regarding your online store, always make sure that user navigation from a consumer's perspective is easy and secure.

With online spending projected by Forrester Research, Inc., to reach $370 billion globally by 2017[8], it's hard to ignore the value of selling online. Whether you are based in rural Oklahoma or the bustling streets of Brooklyn, your online store has the potential to have a global audience. How you capture this audience depends on your online marketing efforts, however. Among the various ways in which you can do this is social media. Having been around since 1994, social media no longer constitute a new trend that retailers should be aware of. Instead, social media should be recognized as established interactive experiences that allow merchants to exchange information within virtual communities and networks—reaching both current and potential customers.

Social Media in Today's Retail Marketplace

Over the years, there has been an ongoing debate as to how social media deliver value to small businesses. Much has been said about the lack of measureable results generated by social media, specifically in the independent arena. According to "2013 Social Media 300: Ranking E-Retail's Leaders in Social Media Marketing and Commerce" from *Internet Retailer Magazine*[9], however, refuting this claim relies heavily on proving that small businesses can in fact find success and generate sales using social media as part of

EXPERT SPOTLIGHT

In addition to having your own website, many independent retailers have found success expanding their product assortment on websites that include Amazon.com, eBay, and Sears.com. These sites have unique selling platforms that collectively generate millions of web visitors each day. With this in mind, it may make sense to also expand your online presence to incorporate these online avenues.

Skip McGrath is a professional eBay and Amazon seller who is widely recognized as an industry expert in selling on both of these websites. Below, he shares his insight on how independent retailers can benefit from applying their sales strategy to include selling on Amazon, eBay, and Sears.

"It used to be a store could open a website and get traffic, but the world of Google has changed; and today it is very difficult for a small shopping site to get any traction with search engines. However, online selling sites such as Amazon, eBay, and Sears.com already have traffic comprised of customers looking for things to buy. Adding one or more of these avenues can have an immediate effect on a retailer's sales.

As you look to get started in exploring these avenues, you should consider the following. To start, eBay used to be king of the mountain when it came to small sellers looking for a way to expand online. But eBay has changed and is no longer as welcoming to smaller sellers. eBay is still the place to sell used and vintage goods, but Amazon has grabbed market share when it comes to new merchandise. And Amazon welcomes new sellers and gives them great support. Sears has also entered the game and is expanding rapidly. But Amazon is still the best place to start.

One more thing to think about is the potential for new customers you can gain through these selling avenues. If you have a store in a small town or a shopping mall, you are exposed to thousands of potential customers, but when you expand online, its like having a store in a city with a population of a hundred million or more."[11]

McGrath shares additional insight on selling on eBay, Amazon and Sears on his website www.SkipMcGrath.com.

their strategies. Leaders on the list include Petflow.com, Fab.com, and Coastal.com—with retail giants such as Walmart, Target, and Best Buy not even making the top 100.

"PetFlow.com brings in 30 percent of its total site traffic and overall revenue from social networks—mostly as a result of a laser-like focus on building and maintaining a loyal Facebook fan base and regular posts that speak to their followers' inner pet lover," the guide identified[10]. Also, it stated that Fab.com received 25 percent of its website traffic from social networks, meaning that a quarter of all its online visitors are a direct result of social media engagement.

Athough these online stores are not your traditional Main Street merchants, their success was found strictly using the Internet as their selling platform. Even if you never strive to have more online sales than offline, recognizing the value of blending both strategies to increase your total sales is a good goal to aim for. That said, don't be surprised if your hard work delivers stronger sales online than off. After all, your reach of consumers is much greater on the web than via any storefront ever, and this can only strengthen with the help of social media.

Using social media to increase your online sales certainly makes sense, but Massachusetts-based retail store Jenny Boston, a five-location boutique selling purses, accessories, and other women's fashion apparel in the Boston suburbs, also finds that social media help to bring foot traffic into their stores.

Jenny Boston co-owners Jennifer DeMaria and Kristin Maynard began posting and selling items on Facebook in October 2012. Since then, not only have their online sales exceeded those of their actual physical stores, but they've increased their in-store foot traffic as a result of people picking up their items purchased online and often making a few more purchases once in the boutiques. This type of chain reaction that begins on a social media site such as Facebook—which has 1.5 billion plus users and growing—is proof that selling online. using social media, and having a physical storefront truly go hand in hand.

* * *

Although aiming to gain store attention and sales should always be your goal, it's easy for independent retailers to feel as if they can't

do it all. Your to-do lists are long, and adding yet another responsibility to your plate often can seem overwhelming.

"Study after study has shown that small businesses believe in
the power of social media but don't participate actively for two reasons. This includes not having time and not knowing what to say,"
explains chief operating officer Suzy Teele of SnapRetail.com.[12]

SnapRetail, an online marketing company that provides marketing solutions specifically for independent retailers, demonstrates
that automated marketing solutions can help busy retailers to
actively participate in social media while saving time and delivering prewritten content. Teele continues:

> Selecting a marketing automation solution that provides
> prewritten content can deliver ease while being effective for
> retailers. When a retailer has interesting, clever, or mean-
> ingful social media posts at their fingertips and can browse
> and schedule a month's worth or more at a time, the anxiety
> about social media goes away, and the retailer successfully
> engages with their customers instead.[13]

Using strong, engaging content on your social media posts is an
important piece of the social media puzzle. More important is getting engaged in social media to begin with. Without participating
in these key consumer virtual communities, you are missing out
on opportunities to communicate with your customers while also
willingly allowing your competition to gain more attention and,
ultimately, sales that could be yours.

Ed Cleary, publisher of the website Retail TouchPoints, believes
that independent retailers should not neglect social media—no

RETAIL TIP

SnapRetail offers prewritten social media posts for retailers to choose from, offering quick, timely, and effective social media posts for them to engage their customers with. SnapRetail also offers images to accommodate your posts, increasing your user experience and social media success.

Below is an example of what SnapRetail's social media gallery looks like. Keep in mind that when visible online and in color, this user page becomes clearer and easier to navigate.

matter how busy or stretched for time they think they may be. Cleary says:

> Independent retailers have great opportunities to share what is going on in their stores both online and via social media. I see way too many small retailers that have fantastic in-store experiences, but you would never know that unless you are physically in their stores. Developing an online communication plan, including an e-mail marketing list and using social media, allows retailers to share their stories, personal messages, product news, and more on a consistent basis. Consistency is key here, allowing stores to remain top of mind for their customers.[14]

Echoing Cleary on this point are Rich Kizer and Georganne Bender, internationally recognized retail experts and keynote speakers who spend their days researching best practices for retailers. Moreover, Kizer and Bender emphasize the value of reaching your target audience with an authentic voice.

> Here's the thing about social media: it's free to use, but it requires an investment of time, which can often translate to money—after all, time *is* money. We've always considered social media no different than an online party that requires constant attention from you, the store owner or store team, which translates to the store's personality itself. You need to engage daily on social media and not neglect your party goers, aka customers. While there are all sorts of companies and apps that offer you the ability to preplan posts and

communicate via social media with your customers, there is nothing like doing it yourself. Your fans and followers want to communicate with *you*.[15]

A key takeaway from Kizer and Bender's thoughts on social media is to always react, respond, and reply to any social media comments, posts, questions, or other activity shared with you or your store via social media. Kizer and Bender suggest setting aside half an hour a day to check your social media sites, allowing you to do the following:

1. *Listen*. Read what's being said.
2. *Interact*. Respond to comments.
3. *React*. Answer questions and respond to complaints.
4. *Sell*. You can push merchandise about every fifth post. Remember, its *social* media, not a catalog listing of what you sell.[16]

In addition to Kizer and Bender's tips on being engaged on social media, SnapRetail believes in a rule it has taglined as the *70-20-10 rule*. This indicates that 70 percent of your social media experience should be engaging content (e.g., fun facts, expert advice, questions), 20 percent should be shared content (e.g., other customers, partner stores, vendor information, etc.), and 10 percent should be related to the products, sales, or other information about your store. As SnapRetail's Suzy Teele tells me, "This is the right balance to build a strong, responsive following."[17]

Part of finding the right balance also means identifying which social media channels make the most sense for your audience.

Facebook and Pinterest tend to generate the most linkbacks that lead to consumer purchases, with Twitter, Instagram, and Google+ also used to engage your target consumer audience. Remember that despite this diverse range of social media options, there is trusted support for those who simply don't have the time to manage them effectively. SnapRetail.com and BoutiqueWindow.com are both companies to consider, with countless apps also available to help you manage your social media communication.

EXPERT SPOTLIGHT

Social media offers a way for retailers large or small to connect with customers on a daily basis. Among the top social media sites for retailers to do this is Facebook, where frequent users are reportedly logging on to their accounts as many as 10 times per day.

Boutique Window is a marketing platform designed uniquely for independent retailers to share product images and more via social media. Cofounder, Ella Wirtz, encourages retailers to incorporate Facebook into marketing strategies as a way to stay engaged with customers while also pushing selling opportunities.

"Facebook is the perfect platform to share pictures of new product arrivals, last-minute sales, special events, store promotions, and more. Furthermore, keep your Facebook updates fresh by sharing interesting advice, product tips, and seasonal recommendations along with the product images you post. Your pictures are key, however. This is what will get your customers most excited."[18]

Finally, in the spirit of reaching thousands and aiming to increase your sales by thousands, we've identified a top 10 list of resources to help you in your online sales and social media initiatives. Please note that the recommended resources are listed alphabetically.

1. *Boutique Window, BoutiqueWindow.com* Showcase merchandise on Facebook, Twitter, Pinterest, and your website through Boutique Window's photo editing tools and online publishing capabilities. This savvy online marketing company was created entirely for independent merchants, helping you reach more customers, gain more sales, and increase store visibility.

2. *Do It In Person, DoItInPerson.com* This online event plat-form allows retailers and other businesses to manage and promote their events in one convenient place.

3. *Internet Retailer Magazine, InternetRetailer.com* This digital and print publication produces a flagship maga-zine as well as four annual research guides specifically on the subject of selling online. Lean on their free online blog for additional news pertaining to e-commerce, social media, mobile marketing, and more.

4. *Retail TouchPoints, RetailTouchPoints.com* Gain timely articles on retaining customers in the diverse world of multitouch retailing from this free, subscription-based resource. Retail TouchPoints is designed for retail execu-tives but shares valuable reports and industry news so that retailers small and large can learn more.

5. *Shipwire, Shipwire.com* If storage becomes an issue and your one or more storefronts outgrow your online sell-

ing inventory, Shipwire can support you in storing your product, providing fast and reliable shipping, managing your distributions and deliveries, and much, much more. Their ultimate goal is to help you save time, cost, and complexity—which any independent retailer knows is a good goal to have.

6. *Shopify, Shopify.com* Thanks to e-commerce template options, retailers can introduce an online store in seven easy, hassle-free steps from Shopify. In addition, the company's blog and Ecommerce University share a tremendous amount of valuable information and news about selling online and engaging in social media that all retailers can learn from.

7. *SnapRetail, SnapRetail.com* Communicate with your customers with automated, prewritten social media, e-mail marketing, and general store communications content. In addition, gain access to countless images and other promotional materials provided by SnapRetail specifically for independent retailers. SnapRetail also offers its users a management calendar to track store events, online promotions, e-mail blasts, social media updates, and more.

8. *Soldsie, Soldsie.com* Soldsie allows retailers to bring their web stores to Facebook. It's easy to use, fun for customers to engage, and helps to turn social media communication into sales. Although there are other options to consider, including Beetailer.com, Soldsie is a retailer favorite.

9. *Vine, Vine.com.* This Twitter-owned mobile app reached 40 million users in August 2013 and continues to grow

every day. Used to incorporate videos into your online messaging, Vine allows customers and retailers alike to engage via video, with the opportunity to share a behind-the-scenes look at your store, offer product how-tos, share industry updates, and more. Essentially, it brings your personality alive and allows your customers to become even more connected to your brand and your business. It's also a great way to challenge your customers via contests online to share their own videos with you.

10. *Wishpond, Wishpond.com* Wishpond is an app that makes it easy to run a group offer or social media contest to drive sales and traffic to your website or store with coupons and other special offers via Facebook, Twitter, Pinterest, your website, and mobile devices. Seventy-thousand plus businesses use this with trust, and their support is constantly evolving with retailers in mind.

Engaging online as part of your brick-and-mortar strategy is a vital part in both reaching and keeping today's consumers—whether online or in your physical storefront.

* * *

Although incorporating an online presence into your business is vital in today's modern marketplace, it's also important to take part in buy-local and shop-independent initiatives. In Chapter 10, we'll discuss this in more detail and identify ways in which you can incorporate this practice into your business and community.

Action Guide

Creating an online store and using social media to help promote it can add value and visibility to your business. Another way to increase your odds of gaining more awareness online is through content marketing.

Content marketing is intended to attract and keep customer attention though the use of words—content—applied to your product descriptions, company profile, marketing strategies, and all other written communications. Essentially, content marketing supports businesses in their sale and brand identity, creating an avenue of communication in which customers engage. Also, content marketing overlaps into how online search engines, such as Google, rank your website in online searches. Collectively, these reasons offer retailers a valuable excuse to make content marketing a priority for their businesses.

Using the following product description as an example, create your own product descriptions for no less than five products currently being sold in your store. Whether you have an online business or not, identifying a savvy, precise, and engaging way to communicate details about your products can help you to stand out among other merchants and in the eyes of consumers.

Example: Product description for classic white ladies crew-neck
   T-shirt
Description: 100 percent cotton, side-seamed and cap-sleeved
   T-shirt with a contoured fit that shapes the natural curves
   of a woman's body, positioning about four inches below the
   waistline.

Prior to identifying your product descriptions as complete, have at least three other people review them. Show them the descriptions without pictures to complement them; then show them the product pictures or actual product only after they have read the description. Using this as a test for your content marketing, have your subjects identify whether your product descriptions accurately describe the actual images you show them.

10

Taking Part in Shop-Local Initiatives

However beautiful the strategy, you should
occasionally look at the results.

—*Winston Churchill (1874–1965),*
former Prime Minister of United Kingdom

Remember that Astoria, New York, retailer we mentioned earlier in this book? Well, Mackenzi Farquer, a retail store owner for over seven years, suggests that being a visible member of your local community is key to staying relevant and profitable in a crowded marketplace:

My number one rule for survival is to stay visible within your community. By embedding yourself in the fabric of your local marketplace, you help to make customers feel responsible for your success or failure. Furthermore, it's important to do what big-box stores either do not or cannot do, such as providing free delivery on select purchases, accepting every credit card, having no credit card minimums, and going to great lengths to deliver memorable, strong customer service.[1]

As a seasoned store owner, Farquer's insight is something to be considered. One way to become engrained in your local marketplace is to participate in a buy-local campaign.

Understanding Buy-Local Campaigns

Buy-local campaigns are defined by the American Independent Business Alliance (AMIBA) as organized campaigns that engage local citizens and businesses to shift their spending habits to benefit independent business owners.

Jeff Milchen, codirector of AMIBA, explains that communities and independent business owners can gain sales, support, and attention by introducing a buy-local campaign in their communities:

When properly structured and sustained over time by grassroots organizations, buy-local campaigns are making a big impact in shifting culture and spending habits. For example, in a January 2013 survey by the Institute for Local Self-Reliance, independent businesses in communities with campaigns by such groups reported an average annual revenue increase of 8.6 percent, compared with 3.4 percent among independents in other communities. This was the fifth straight year their annual survey showed such a differential. While they don't prove cause and effect, these surveys are among several strong pieces of evidence that buy-local campaigns truly make an impact for independent business owners.[2]

Moreover, Milchen points out that these surveys only count campaigns that define *local* as local ownership and independently owned. He continues:

> The countless "buy-local" campaigns started by municipalities or groups unwilling to distinguish between local ownership and mere physical location almost universally fade away without making an impact.[3]

Using the figure in the following sidebar, you should be able to identify year-to-year sales increases among independent businesses who actively engaged in buy-local campaigns run by independent business alliances such as AMIBA.

With sales success a clear advantage of incorporating a buy-local campaign into your own community, the question remains how you can do so effectively. Milchen says that being clear in your communications and goals is critical in your planning efforts:

> Be clear in every communication that you plan when developing a buy-local and independent shopping campaign. It only takes one person in a meeting with the idea of a campaign that includes "shop your local Walmart" to do great harm. Be sure to emphasize locally owned indepen-

RETAIL TIP

The American Independent Business Alliance, also recognized as AMIBA, helps retailers and communities create and manage "buy local" and "buy independent" campaigns. Below, you can see how sales were impacted among independent businesses who participated in these types of campaigns from 2010 through 2012.

Do Buy Independent / Buy Local Campaigns Make a Difference?

Year-to-year sales increases among independent businesses

Communities with campaigns run by Independent Business Alliances® / Local First Networks

No Independent Business Alliance / Local First Network

Data: Institute for Local Self-Reliance
Graphic: American Independent Business Alliance
Graph source file: amiba.net/buy-local-campaigns

dent businesses in your messaging. While directly critiquing chains or absentee-owned businesses is not essential, your audience should understand that you intend *local* to mean local ownership and control, not merely location.[4]

Fortunately for busy retailers and community leaders looking to introduce a buy-local campaign into their communities, a vast range of help is available. Among the first steps you should take is to contact AMIBA to see if anyone else in your community has already inquired about an organized buy-local campaign. Being linked to this person or group of people can help you in organizing a like-minded group of individuals to work together with the same goal of supporting independent businesses in mind.

Next, obtain a free copy of AMIBA's "Guide to Creating a Buy-Local Campaign," which delivers how-to steps on getting started, organizing partnerships, leveraging local relationships, sharing your message, and more. The guide, available in both print and digital formats, can be obtained at http://www.amiba.net/about /primer-form. This 12-page overview of kick-starting a buy-local campaign contains details on creating your own community logo, ideas to generate media support, and insights into incorporating your buy-local campaign as a nonprofit with the goal of becoming a 501c6 organization (an Internal Revenue Service designation). AMIBA also can support you with free guidance through every step of the way to ensure that you not only save time but also avoid unnecessary expenses.

Milchen encourages people interested in starting their own buy-local campaigns to take full advantage of what is readily available already. "Don't waste time and money reinventing the wheel,"[5] he explains. With a trusted resource such as AMIBA having spent 12+ years gathering and refining best practices, materials, and tools available to communities and independent business owners, it makes sense to save some time by leaning on AMIBA for help in achieving your buy-local goals.

In addition to AMIBA, other resources are available to you to help you create a buy-local and buy-independent campaign. Among them is the Business Alliance for Local Living Economies (BALLE), which is focused on creating prosperity by connecting leaders and solutions in local economies.

Among the benefits that BALLE offers for retailers and their community leaders are the *BALLE calculators*. Through these calculators, you are able to identify how self-reliant your town is in food, what missing opportunities may exist for job creation, and where you can find the nearest bank or credit union. Although the answers to these questions may come quickly to you, the collective analysis of these questions and countless others can help retailers and communities identify weaknesses, strengths, and opportunities. As BALLE explains, "Calculating missed opportunities for revenue and job creation is invaluable for living economic development."[6] For retailers in particular, this includes providing a better sense of opportunities for expansion and understanding the more profitable markets in your local community.

Combining the efforts of AMIBA and BALLE as official partners, Shift Your Shopping is one more way to get involved in sharing the message of shopping local with your community. More than 160 organizations have united already to encourage consumers to shift their shopping from big-box to independent retailers, a considerable accomplishment from this grassroots campaign. The collective efforts of BALLE and AMIBA and more than 160 local organizations that together equal more than 38,000 local businesses support the Shift Your Shopping campaign. This campaign encourages customers to buy from locally owned businesses—including restaurants, service-based retailers such as dry cleaners, chiropractic offices, and brick-and-mortar merchants. It's their belief that "a single merchant has the ability to shift attitudes or consumer spending. But by building strength in numbers, we can create broad support for independent businesses and advocate for their interests."[7]

Finding Success Through Small-Business Saturday

In addition to supporting consistent buy-local and other independent business campaigns, the increasingly popular Small Business Saturday campaign that was founded in 2010 by American Express is something all retailers should embrace—whether they accept American Express in their stores or not. This one-day event takes place the Saturday following Thanksgiving, although the messaging and campaign efforts are recognized as "Shop Small" all year round.

2013's Small Business Saturday showed that customers who were aware of this highlighted day spent $5.7 billion, a 3.6 percent increase from 2012. This study, completed by the National Federation of Independent Businesses and American Express Research, also confirms that in just four short years, customers have adopted Small Business Saturday as something they want to support.[8]

"Customers are making Small Business Saturday part of their holiday shopping traditions," Susan Sobbott, president of American Express OPEN states. "Our 2013 Small Business Saturday saw a continuation of this growing trend as communities around the country came together to celebrate local businesses and helped drive consumers to Shop Small on the day."[9]

In addition to the in-store sales and local community attention that this campaign generates, there was a 65 percent increase in Twitter engagement revolving around Small Business Saturday from 2012 to 2013 alone. This type of growth, combined with more than 3.3 million Facebook users having liked the official Small Business Saturday Facebook page, only reinforces that shopping small and shopping local is here to stay.[10]

Washington, DC–based professional writer and consumer Amy Knebel first heard of Small Business Saturday in 2011, a year after its introduction to the marketplace. Since then, Knebel has actively participated as a customer supporting independent retailers on Small Business Saturday, making it a tradition among herself and her friends to frequent local businesses to kick off their holiday shopping. Knebel explains:

> I love the Old Town Alexandria Boutique District, which I live close to, and can't imagine not having all the fantastic boutiques, restaurants, and independent businesses that make up this neighborhood. For me, supporting Small Business Saturday is my way of saying thank you to the many businesses and their owners for helping to make my everyday life that much more interesting and fun.[11]

Actively engaging in multiple buy-local and shop-small campaigns not only is becoming more popular to do as a retailer but also is becoming more recognized and respected from a consumer perspective. This reason alone should be enough of a push to make you want to get involved because supporting your customers always should be a goal. Although participating in multiple buy-local campaigns, such as your own local community campaign, Shift Your Shopping, and Small Business Saturday, may seem like an unlikely first step for a busy retailer, we hope that you will make it a priority as time passes. The resources available to you are plentiful, and the success of a well-executed campaign is measured in sales—something we're certain any retailer can appreciate.

To recap the resources identified throughout this chapter, please refer to the following list:

* American Independent Business Alliance (AMIBA), www.amiba.net
* Business Alliance for Local Living Economies (BALLE), www.BeALocalist.org
* Institute for Local Self-Reliance, www.ilsr.org
* Shift Your Shopping, www.shiftyourshopping.org
* Shop Small and Small Business Saturday, www.shopsmall.com

Introducing Commerce and Charity

Shop-local, buy-local, and shop-small campaigns are not the only familiar movements taking place in retail right now. Commerce and charity are increasingly becoming a familiar duo, with the holiday season being a particularly popular time of year for retailers big and small to request donations for their charities of choice. Virginia-based Causetown.org believes that consumers don't necessarily want to change their shopping behaviors to give to charity, which is why donating a percentage of purchases made is becoming a preferred way for customers to give back.

As a consumer, you have likely experienced the combination of commerce and charity yourself while checking out at a grocery store or other big-box retailer. Have you ever wondered how this can be applied to independent merchants, though? Until recently, a collection jar with a slot for loose change or the occasional folded-up bill was the most likely avenue for independent retailers to participate in collecting for a charity of their choice. Now, however, organizations such as Causetown.org allow local businesses to raise awareness and funds by partnering with a nonprofit. The goal is to support independent businesses by promoting events, offering promotional materials, handling sales tracking, managing fund distribution, and more—all to help support charities.

Dan McCabe, one of the founders of Causetown.org, explains, "Research shows that 83 percent of customers want to buy products that benefit a cause."[12] Keeping this in mind, combining your business with a charity of your choice is another movement you should consider for your store.

· · ·

Finally, in Chapter 11 we'll look ahead at the future of independent retail and how your participation as a business owner can affect not only your singular success or failure but also the economy at large.

Action Guide

Ready to make your community and locally owned businesses stand out in consumer minds? To kick-start your efforts, form a steering committee that can help you launch a buy-local campaign in your town.

1. *Introduce the idea of a buy-local campaign to local business owners and key decision makers in your community.* Be prepared to identify the benefits of a buy-local campaign and to explain what it would take to get one started. Using the resources identified throughout this chapter, you can confidently suggest resources to help you launch a campaign.

2. *Aim to gather a mix of business owners and influential community leaders to be a part of your committee.* Combining the minds, resources, and community reach of a diverse steering committee can help you accomplish your buy-local campaign planning more effectively. Ideally, you should have long-time business owners—community leaders such as your economic director, mayor, or alderman—and highly regarded individuals on your committee who either volunteer or work with other organizations that reach a lot of consumers. Between 7 and 12 members would be ideal, although a few less or a few more still can work to deliver a strong committee.

3. *Identify a date and a list of future dates to meet as a group to begin your efforts in planning for a buy-local campaign.* During these scheduled meetings, be sure to clearly identify who is responsible for what, with deadlines clearly stated, to ensure follow through. Having a leader or two on your steering committee can help everyone to stay on track with their individual responsibilities as well.

Once a committee has been identified and each member is committed to creating a buy-local campaign with the same goals in mind, be sure to lean on the resources identified in this chapter to help you in moving forward. Through your combined efforts, you can establish a strong campaign within your own community to increase independent business visibility and sales while also enhancing your local customers' community experience.

11

A Crystal Ball for
Independent Retailers

The best way to predict your future is to create it.

—*Peter F. Drucker (1909–2005), author, consultant, professor*

I F SOMEONE had told you when you were just embarking on your career path that you would become a store owner, would you have believed him or her? The reality is that retail isn't a job many retailers set out to do. "I didn't go chasing a dream of being a business owner, particularly a retail store owner. This dream chased me,"[1] Kimberly Efseaff, of Bon Bijoux Girly Boutique in Del Mar, California, told us.

Having heard similar stories from countless other retailers, we know that retail isn't always the job they have dreamed of—whereas others feel just the opposite and consider owning their own store a dream come true. "I can't imagine living my life any other way than how I do now, which is being in my store seven days a week. It's something I've always wanted to do and am thrilled to actually be doing it,"[2] Chicago-based store owner Angela Gianfrancesco said.

The Future of Independent Retail

Whether you fall into the category of an accidental retailer or a retailer by intent, the future of this dynamic business has a lot in store for you. Jason Richelson, founder and CEO of ShopKeep POS, believes that there is a lot for independent merchants to look forward to:

> I have five predictions for the future of retail, beginning with the fact that the cloud is here to stay and Windows is dead. Over the next three to five years, the cloud will really come of age in retail, and Windows-based POS (point of sale) and other operations will disappear. This will kick-start in April 2014 when Microsoft will stop supporting XP, which will render hundreds of thousands of Windows POS systems out of PCI (payment card industry) compliance. Retailers will have to start thinking about upgrading their existing technology—with the cloud being the obvious option. The vast adoption of iOS and Android will also drive this shift, along with the proliferation of mobile devices.
>
> Next, I believe we're going to see handheld registers that allow staff to help customers on the shop floor and then ring them up right there, instead of having to line up to get to the counter. The type of handheld register that has been

proven to work for Apple, Nordstrom, and Barneys will ultimately come to small stores, I believe; and as a result, there will no longer be a reason to have a counter to process transactions. That space can be freed up for other uses, like displays or more floor space.

Also, and again referencing the cloud, I believe that small retailers will be able to access data similar to how big-box retailers have been for years. The cloud has leveled the playing field and lowered the price point for this type of information collection and analysis, effectively democratizing data. The world of customer, product, and sales analysis that only existed for the Walmarts or Starbucks of this world now exists for anyone who wants it. In 2014, access to data will be the equalizer for small businesses. The next differentiator will be knowing how to use it.

With these data and combined with POS technology, I also believe retailers will be able to better identify where their marketing dollars should be spent. Small businesses are expected to spend more than half of their marketing budgets on their own assets in 2014, including their websites, e-mail marketing campaigns, and social media channels. This will be driven by two things; the availability of cost-effective online tools and the ability to act on their own customer data. POS technology has fundamentally changed the customer interaction. Instead of a customer handing over cash and walking away, you are gathering information and building a profile of that customer that can be used to market to them. Small retailers will start to take advantage of this, and we will see the marketing dollars follow.

Finally, over time, we are going to see a variety of business services start to integrate with the POS system. Different apps a retailer might use to run their store including loyalty, CRM (customer resource management), accounting, e-mail marketing, delivery, social media, payroll, mobile payments, and more will plug in to the back end of POS, allowing retailers to use multiple tools in an integrated fashion. As a result, merchants can then operate and report on all these systems from a single view, with the most important thing at the center—which is what is happening at the cash register. This is the future for retailers.[3]

Richelson's expansive prediction of where independent retail is heading is—in our opinion—right on. Thanks to the cloud and data-collecting technologies that have advanced in recent years on the retail scene, small retailers can finally become more competitive within their local and global marketplaces. These opportunities for independent retailers can create a domino effect of good, or bad, results based on what kind of growth, change, and customer care they introduce to their stores.

Vend CEO Vaughan Rowsell shares his thoughts on the future of retail as well, specifically discussing how point-of-sale (POS) systems can help retailers to leverage more sales and better manage their businesses. You'll find that much of what Rowsell says is also supported by Richelson's thoughts, reinforcing the idea that the future of retail is developing at a steady pace among leading industry players.

Web-based POS is ground breaking in every respect for independent retailers. First off, a web-based POS lowers the barrier to entry. Via subscription-based web software, independent retailers can now afford the sophisticated tools and real-time analytics that big retailers have been leveraging for years. Also, small startups can get a POS for less than it costs to buy two pizzas a month. But there are other, even more exciting facets to web-based POS, which are add-ons and custom solutions.

Just as retailers can now customize the retail experience on their shop floors, they can also customize their POS software to exactly fit their needs. Web-based software (also called *software as a service*, or SAAS) is often complementing other software, allowing retailers to truly take control of their retail operations. An example of this would be for a retailer to integrate their POS system with their accounting software. This not only saves them hours of administration time every week, but also spares them possible external bookkeeping expenses or timely double-entry procedures on multiple spreadsheets or in multiple software accounts.

This said, POS can be even more customizable than this. If you own a hair salon, for example, you need to be able to keep track of your products and your appointments—two very different details of your business yet equally important. With SAAS solutions, this is easy. You simply find an add-on that integrates appointment software with your POS system, and away you go.

Finally, other solutions can be cherry picked as you need them to help manage your unique business specifically. Want to spare your customers the crazy queues during the holiday season? Integrate your POS system with a self-checkout app so that customers can ring themselves up and pay via their smartphones. Want to take orders and accept payments in advance at your café? There's an add-on for that too. In the future, there will likely be an app for anything you can think of as well.[4]

An app for everything is certainly a prediction we can expect to become reality, but what about the future of retail beyond technology?

The Future Beyond Technology

Portable cash registers, cloud-based data collection, instant app additions, and other technology solutions undoubtedly will play a big role in the future of retail. This said, there is something to be said for good old-fashioned customer care. Supporting this idea is Camille Candella, group marketing manager for Emerald Expositions:

> Today's customers are more educated than ever before, and they have access to more stores than ever before. As a result, customers are becoming more selective in what they want to buy and where they want to buy it. For independent retailers, I believe this will position them to build stronger clientele by giving them more personalized attention and really listening to their needs. One way to do this is to keep products fresh based on what your customers are telling you. Unlike big-box stores, smaller merchants can react faster to customer demands and often receive inventory sooner

based on smaller quantity needs. This certainly plays to the advantage of independent retailers and can help them have more success in their total store sales as well.[5]

Reacting to customers on a faster, more focused scale is unarguably a trend that retailers will need to embrace and likewise one that consumers will begin to demand. Publisher Bill McNulty of Sumner Communications, Inc., shares this prediction, anticipating consumer expectations among all retailers to increase in years to come:

> The harsh reality is that over the next few years in any type of business, anything you try that is poorly executed is going to have significant struggles. The consumer expectation bar has risen across the board at an alarming rate. If you give shoppers a reason to walk through your door, they will. However, if you go half speed and hope everything will work itself out, you're in for an uphill climb. The market speaks loud and clear, and it is never wrong. While this may seem like a huge challenge, more than ever before, small retailers have the ability to change buying behaviors instead of simply reacting to them.
>
> Retailers are the first and last line of defense for customer service. Technology is what it is and can be a great tool for marketing, but self-checkout and single-click buying will never replace face-to-face relationship building for an overwhelming percentage of your customers. Offering fantastic customer service, going the extra mile for a customer, and adding a personal touch to every transaction are things only you and your team can do. People remember kindness, and

they remember great service. Understand that your customer, deep down, would really prefer to buy locally—from you—than from your nearest big-box neighbor. Use this to your advantage, and do something to reward that behavior.[6]

McNulty's opinion on supporting customers with exceptional customer care no matter how much new technology is introduced is something all retailers should pay attention to. While iPads and other modern technologies should have a place in your store, it's important not to lose sight of how strong customer service can have an impact on your business—and ultimately, your retail future. In fact, as other merchants embrace technology entirely and dismiss these presumed old-fashioned selling techniques, you should leverage the power of combining these tactics to maximize your store's full potential. Jewelry retailer Angela Gianfrancesco has plans to do to just that:

> I love that modern conveniences like point of sale and e-mail marketing solutions make my job so much easier, but I never want to forget why I believe customers shop at my store. It's not just the ease of a customer checkout experience that they enjoy but rather the entire experience of my store. I know that my personality along with my team's has a lot to do with this, and I don't want to neglect just how meaningful this is to my business.[7]

Gianfrancesco offers a good reminder for all merchants, pointing out that part of your store is in fact your personality. As you embark or continue on your retail journey, always remember that your personality affects your business, plain and simple. Moreover, remember that your employees are a reflection of your business and can affect your store's success and sales as well.

* * *

With black-and-white data increasingly becoming more accessible to retailers and technology becoming an expected addition to retail storefronts, merchants should embrace the changes taking place both online and offline when it comes to managing and marketing their retail stores. Delaying the incorporation of these technologies and modern amenities can push retailers years behind their competitors, making their race to *finally* catch up nearly impossible once they're ready. To help avoid this long-winded journey, make your future more predictable by welcoming the realities of modern retail into your business model today.

When Retail Isn't in Your Future

Despite what the economy, trends in retail, and even your own personal goals may be for the future, some retailers may get to a point where they want or need to sell their store. This decision doesn't need to be perceived as a bad one but rather simply as a step in a different direction. Often retailers who need to move out of state, want to retire, or have other goals in mind choose to sell their businesses as a way to move forward. Group general manager Curtis Kroeker of BizBuySell.com and BizQuest.com shares his thoughts on how selling your business may be your best decision yet:

There are many factors that go into determining if a business sale is right for you. The first step is to objectively assess your business as a sale prospect. Prospective buyers will do extensive research before signing on the dotted line, so make sure that you thoroughly examine your financials, infrastructure, staffing, and even clientele to determine if your business will be covered. If there are issues in any of these areas, be sure to at least create an action plan to guide the new owner, but you'll better position your business for a successful sale if you address these issues prior to selling. This will help to draw in more prospective buyers and improve your chances for a higher sales price down the line.

In addition, it's important to remember that selling a business is a personal decision. Make sure to analyze your motivations for selling to ensure that it is the right step for you. Why do you want to sell? Are you burnt out? Looking to do the next thing? Having health problems? Simply ready for that well-deserved retirement? There are countless reasons you may be considering a sale. Determining why you want to get out will help you to set your desired time line and goals for the sale. This will, among other things, help you decide how to trade off sale speed and sale price— two goals that are often somewhat at odds. Also be sure to outline your postsale plan. You may be retiring, using the money for another venture, or even staying with the company in a managerial capacity. Defining these after-sale interests will help you determine if you are ready to sell and design a sale approach that fits your motivations.

Next, if you believe selling your business may be in your future, start planning for this now. The best retailers are always working to improve business value. If you have a sale in mind from the very start, it ensures that you are always thinking about how to maximize value and will be in a better position when the time comes to sell. However, if you haven't been thinking this way, don't despair. There's still time. Just don't put off this way of thinking any longer. Positioning your business to maximize your sale outcome will take time.

To start preparing your business for sale, put together a presale action plan. The goal of this plan is to get all the improvements done for which you have the energy and capability. Doing so will ensure that your business is in its best shape when it hits the market. The next step is collecting and organizing necessary documentation. Sooner or later, prospective buyers are going to want to see "just the facts" on paper. This usually includes at least three years of financial statements that will help to prove your business's worth. Next, start assembling your sales team. Selling a business is not an extracurricular activity; it is a full-time job. Experienced sellers leverage the help of qualified business brokers, appraisers, accountants, and attorneys to handle the many details of a successful sale. This allows them to focus on maintaining or accelerating business performance while it is on the market—nothing sells a business better than strengthening financials. With a good team in place, you'll be well positioned to price your business right, prepare your for-sale marketing materials, and much more.

Finally, don't be intimidated by the thought of selling your business, but don't underestimate what it takes to sell a business either. The proper presale preparation can mean the difference between a successful sale and long, drawn-out frustration. These tips will help you to get started, but there are countless more details that you should consider. To learn more, you can check out our full BizBuySell Guide to Selling Your Small Business at http://www.bizbuysell.com /seller/guide/selling-a-business/.[8]

Your future in retail doesn't have to end, or start, in any traditional way. Selling your business may not be your goal today, but knowing upfront that it might be one day is what your takeaway should be here. After all, you want to build a business that is worth something, don't you? Whether you plan to pass your business down through generations, hope to sell it one day for a gain, or simply hope to work until you don't want to work anymore, planning ahead and creating a strategy for your business should remain top of mind. You may be your own boss, after all, but that doesn't mean that you can predict your outcome. That responsibility is left in the hands of consumers.

Parting Words from Jason Prescott

It used to be expected that revolutions in retail occurred every couple of years—or maybe even decades. In a very short historical time frame, we moved from small street independents to department stores yielding massive conglomerates to e-commerce behemoths. A new dynamic paradigm has created a massive shift to what can easily be stated as a customer-centric revolution. As technology molds every movement and investment retailers make, the most significant investment that must be made is knowing and understanding the granularity of your potential and existing customer base. As a result, a retail storefront must be seen as much more than a storefront or place where services and merchandise are merely transacted. The store needs to become the battlefield where knowledge acquisition of your customers must occur.

To help retailers move forward with this state of mind, merchants must realize and embrace the fact that data are now being transacted at every point. When a shopper enters a store, the day will soon be here where digital displays synch with profiles and Google Glass (a wearable computer with an optical head-mounted display) allowing merchants to access a plethora of information that is constantly gathered and processed by these devices. Credit and debit cards will also become even more meaningful to retailers, with every swipe becoming an opportunity to collect consumer details and shopping trends from companies such as Cardlytics. Furthermore, these details will be able to be shared with other merchants, making a retailer's chance to both collect and share customer contact details more relevant in all their store decisions.

Of course, Facebook, Twitter, Google Places, Yelp, TripAdvisor, and other major influencers will continue to help businesses compete against the Walmarts of the world; but to truly compete, it's the underlying business intelligence-gathering process that will shape the future of retail. Consumers have become the most powerful media force in the world today. They bond together in their similar interests and choose to trot down the path of reviews, referrals, and social buzz; and they advocate what is popular at the moment. If you are going to succeed, you must be focused on not becoming a fad but setting trends and constantly adapting to the dynamic lifestyle changes of those you value most—your customers.

Parting Words from Nicole Leinbach Reyhle

It's competitive in retail, no matter how big or small your store is. Keeping up with customer expectations, market trends, retail changes, and your local community is a nonstop job that demands much more than a traditional 40-hour workweek. That said, retail is an exciting, always evolving, and constantly entertaining business that, as a result, is one you must constantly tend to.

Unlike much of our retail competition, independent merchants do not have human resource, marketing, public relations, or other operational in-house teams that help keep their stores visible and their doors open. Rather than run away from this reality, retailers should tackle this head on to help keep their stores afloat and their businesses successful. Often this means accepting that you simply can't do this alone. It's with this in mind that I believe the future of retail will continue to introduce, and embrace, supporting players to independent merchants. Companies such as SnapRetail, Boutique Vision, Premier Packaging, Vend, Square, Shopify, and many others have come to life as a result of need—and have stayed alive as a result of demand. These external business partners are key contributors that deliver effective support for store operations, marketing, management, and even sales. Without them, independent retailers simply cannot thrive in our competitive retail marketplace. Together, however, independent retailers and their external business partners can have a positive impact on economic growth and customer loyalty for years and years to come.

Conclusion

Throughout this book, you have learned how managing and marketing your retail business requires a diverse range of skills, support, and expertise. Moreover, we have introduced you to countless resources, businesses, organizations, and associations that we hope you will find useful in your individual retail businesses. Collectively, the details we shared are intended to help you in your unique retail journey—and we hope that they will do just that. Whether you are new to retail altogether, have had a store open for countless years, or sell exclusively online, we applaud you for taking the time to learn more to help your business and wish you success as your embark on your retail journey ahead.

APPENDIX A

Resources for
Independent Retailers

THE FOLLOWING list was created to offer you a collective destination to identify the best resources for entrepreneurs and retailers specifically. These businesses, all of which we provide website details for, cover a variety of topics that include where to go to gain small-business loans, companies to help with your retail marketing, educational publications specific to retailers, trade associations to help your niche business, and much, much more. Listed in alphabetical order, these resources should be evaluated uniquely for your niche retail business.

Advanstar, advanstar.com Advanstar is an event and marketing services business that serves retailers through trade shows, publications, and other industry-specific events. Among its trade shows are MAGIC Market Week and ENT International.

American Apparel and Footwear Association, WeWear.org The American Apparel and Footwear Association (AAFA) is a national trade association that represents apparel, footwear, and other sewn-products companies and suppliers. The association has retailer-specific support and offers valuable insight for merchants who sell these product categories.

American Independent Business Alliance, amiba.net This nonprofit organization helps communities and retailers launch and operate buy-local campaigns to support local entrepreneurs, economies, and retailers.

ART Home Furnishings Network, AccessoriesResourceTeam.org ART is a member-based organization in the home furnishings industry that includes retailers, importers, sales representatives, product designers, interior designers, and industry supporters. ART offers its members a forum to learn, network, and gain additional benefits to help their businesses.

ASD Trade Show, ASDonline.com ASD Las Vegas brings the world's widest variety of general merchandise together in one efficient consumer goods trade show. Held biannually in Las Vegas, annually in New York, and annually in Miami, ASD attracts thousands of retailers and suppliers, supporting retail categories that include gift, home, fashion, health and beauty, jewelry, value and variety, toys, and more.

Association of Small Business Development Centers, asbdc-us.org Small Business Development Centers (SBDC) provides retailers and other small business owners in the United States with assistance, education, and consulting to help launch, grow, and manage their unique businesses. SBDC branches often reside on college campuses and may work closely with their local

Chambers of Commerce and other community programs. Go to the SBDC website to locate a center closest to you.

Bank of America, bankofamerica.com Bank of America offers small-business checking with more control and access than many other banks, allowing you to better manage your business dollars. Bank of America also offers a variety of merchant services that may be suited to your unique retail needs.

BizBuySell, BizBuySell.com The Internet's largest marketplace for buying and selling businesses, as well as a resource destination to gain insight into what you need to do to prepare for this possible step in your retail journey. Whether you want to buy or sell a retail store, this is a fantastic resource to refer to.

Bosi DNA, bosidna.com Discover your entrepreneurial insight through this online quiz identifying what type of entrepreneur you are. Once completed, this quiz reveals ways to strengthen your business weaknesses and maximize your business strengths.

Boutique Vision, BoutiqueVision.com Drive traffic and increase sales through customized store signage and other in-store marketing materials from Boutique Vision. The parent company, InnoMark Communications, is one of the leading providers of custom visual merchandising solutions, and Boutique Vision was created uniquely to support small retailers—keeping budget and quality always top of mind.

Boutique Window, BoutiqueWindow.com Showcase your new inventory and other highlighted products through Facebook, Twitter, Pinterest, and your website through Boutique Window's built-in photo editing tools and online marketing management resources.

Bureau of Labor Statistics, http://stats.bls.gov/audience/business.htm
The Bureau of Labor Statistics provides statistics that help
you find new markets for your store and can compare your
business with others in the industry, as well as assess employment costs.

*Business Alliance for Local Living Economies (BALLE), BeALocal-
ist.org* The Business Alliance for Local Living Economies is a
fast-growing alliance of entrepreneurs, business networks, and
local economy funders in North America who aim to gain
prosperity among communities and help independent retailers
and other small-business owners thrive.

BusinessUSA, http://business.usa.gov/ This is a one-stop shop destination for everything related to business in the United States.
Essentially, this is a destination to gain additional resources
for your business.

Cardlytics, Cardlytics.com Through Cardlytics, you can reach
individuals based on their unique purchase history and help
to drive sales to your store, raise promotion awareness, build
loyalty, and more.

Causetown, Causetown.org Causetown helps local, independent
businesses to attract customer attention and encourage sales
through promotions that give a portion of purchases to each
customer's charity of choice. The platform manages all the
details of these transactions, including charity distribution,
allowing community fundraising for independent retailers to
be easy and accessible.

Council of State Retail Associations, CouncilSRA.com The Council of State Retail Associations (CSRA) was organized to
strengthen and support the retail industry, working with

individual state retail association executives as well as directly with retailers. The goal is to help support association members and the retail community at large.

Craft and Hobby Association, CraftAndHobby.org This international, not-for-profit trade association consists of thousands of member companies engaged in the design, manufacture, and retailing of craft and hobby items. The association offers a vast range of resources and benefits to its members and produces a number of events each year.

Crafters' Home, CraftersHome.com Crafters' Home is a membership-based organization that supports independent scrapbook and paper craft retailers, helping to maximize a retailer's relationship with manufacturers and customers. Crafters' offers a variety of benefits to its members that include discounts from vendors and more.

Do It In Person, DoItInPerson.com This online event platform allows retailers and other businesses to manage and promote their events in one convenient place.

Emerald Expositions, EmeraldExpositions.com Formerly Nielsen Expositions, Emerald Expositions is a leading owner and operator of a variety of business-to-business trade shows, most of which cater to retailers. The market categories include general merchandise, apparel, sports, jewelry, furniture, design, and more.

GlobalShop, GlobalShop.org GlobalShop is the world's largest annual event for retail design and shopper marketing, creating a one-stop destination for retailers to connect directly with store fixture companies and other in-store solutions. Global-Shop also offers networking and learning opportunities.

Ideation, IdeationGifts.com Ideation is the premier gift catalog company in the United States that provides catalog and marketing services to independent gift, toy, and fashion retailers nationwide.

Independent Retailer Conference, RetailMinded.com/Retail-Conference The Independent Retailer Conference holds a flagship one-day conference annually and brings its quality and independent retail-specific education onsite to the ASD Trade Show biannually. Known for addressing key issues in the independent retail scene, the Independent Retailer Conference is widely recognized as a must-attend event for independent store owners.

Independent Retailer Magazine, IndependentRetailer.com This monthly publication offers retail advice on wholesale buying and selling, introducing retailers to importers, manufacturers, trade shows, and countless products for their stores.

Internet Retailer Conference and Exhibition, irce.com The Internet Retailer Conference and Exhibition (IRCE) holds a variety of events that discuss key topics for online merchants, introduce industry resources, and share expert information with attendees. The IRCE can be found at select trade shows, where it holds educational tracks specifically discussing e-commerce solutions and other e-commerce education and expertise.

Internet Retailer Magazine, InternetRetailer.com Internet Retailer *Magazine* supports retailers and other businesses with e-commerce intelligence, news, and market support. The publication delivers 12 issues each year and provides additional resources that include newsletters, research guides, and more.

Institute for Local Self-Reliance, ilsr.org The Institute for Local
Self-Reliance works to provide innovative strategies and
timely support to community development, working with
entrepreneurs and community leaders alike. The website offers
a diverse range of information valuable to business owners.

Internal Revenue Service (IRS), http://www.irs.gov/businesses The
IRS hosts small-business tax workshops and webinars and
provides tax-related information for starting, operating, or
closing a business.

iPad Enclosures, iPadEnclosures.com As cloud-based point-of-sale
(POS) and iPad systems become increasingly popular for
retailers, theft of iPads from retailers is also a concern. iPad
Enclosures offers products specifically designed for retailers
and other businesses, allowing you to take control over your
iPad management and vulnerability to theft.

Kabbage, Kabbage.com Kabbage has simplified the process of
getting a business cash advance, allowing retailers to avoid
traditional banks, hidden fees, and unexpected charges while
trying to gain working capital. The company's flexible fund-
ing options allow qualified retailers to gain quick, convenient
access to capital to help their businesses while also making
money transfers easy and straightforward.

Licensing Expo, LicensingExpo.com The Licensing Expo connects
retailers, brands, and manufacturers to entertainment, character, fashion, art, and corporate brand owners to establish
relationships, spot trends, build strategic partnerships, and
secure promotional tie-ins. It is held once a year in Las Vegas.

MAGIC Market Week, MagicOnline.com/Magic-Market-Week
MAGIC Market Week is the largest global market week for

contemporary men's and women's apparel, footwear, and sourcing. Held biannually in Las Vegas, MAGIC attracts fashion buyers and brands from around the world.

Management One, Management-One.com Management One serves independent retailers and other small businesses by helping them get a better return on their investments, including inventory and people. The core services and products surround inventory planning and solutions, helping retailers achieve greater success and sales.

Manufacturer.com Manufacturer.com is the premier global online business-to-business marketplace where buyers and suppliers connect and profit. Billions of dollars of general merchandise, apparel, and fashion accessories are sourced through Manufacturer.com as millions of buyers throughout the world connect directly to suppliers in China, India, the United States, and dozens of other countries.

Minority Business Development Agency (MBDA), MBDA.gov/main /offices This agency funds a network of minority business centers located throughout the nation that provide minority entrepreneurs with one-on-one assistance in marketing, writing business plans, management, technical assistance, and financial planning.

Modalyst, Modalyst.com Retailers can access rising accessory and jewelry designers in this well-crafted cutting-edge online marketplace that showcases products through virtual showrooms. This is a great destination for fashion and accessory-based retailers.

MOO, Moo.com MOO is an online company that offers business cards, postcards, store hangtags, and other print products that are stylish in design. Many of MOO's designs are ready to go, whereas others are available to be customized.

National Hardware Show, NationalHardwareShow.com The National Hardware Show is the premier trade show for the $343 billion U.S. home-improvement and do-it-yourself (DIY) markets. Held annually in Las Vegas, this show caters to retailers in the building, hardware, lawn and garden, pet, home goods, and farm categories, as well as many other retail sectors.

Premier Packaging, RetailPackaging.com Premier Packaging is a leader in custom printing and offers stock, ready-to-ship retail packaging options for retailers that include paper and plastic bags, ribbons, tissue paper, gift boxes, and more.

Reed Expositions, ReedExpo.com Reed Expositions offers a portfolio of more than 500 events in 41 countries, many of which cater to retailers specifically. The website identifies the more than 500 events, allowing you to identify what may be best for your unique retail business.

Retail Adventures Blog, RetailAdventuresBlog.com Internationally recognized retail experts Rich Kizer and Georganne Bender of Kizer & Bender Speaking write this blog, sharing their firsthand retail experiences while also offering retail insight, tips, and more.

RetailMAVENS, RetailMavens.com RetailMAVENS is managed by husband and wife team Paul and Cathy Wagner, who are previous store owners and current retail consultants. Their expertise primarily falls into retail inventory management, and their services are ideal for merchants who want additional hands-on help for their store inventories and planning.

Retail Minded, RetailMinded.com Retail Minded is the nation's only retail lifestyle publisher that supports independent retailers with news, education, and support to help them both in and out of their stores. The quarterly publication *Retail Minded Magazine* is an avenue by which retail-focused groups, associations, and other member-based organizations can help retailers achieve stronger success. Retail Minded caters to all independent retailers and does not eliminate any sector of retail, and it offers an informative free newsletter for independent merchants.

Retail Radio, RetailRadio.biz The right music in a store enhances the store experience and spending behavior. Retail Radio allows merchants to create the ideal atmosphere for their stores and customers, customizing their own in-store radio station and professionally produced commercials for their businesses.

Retail TouchPoints, RetailTouchPoints.com Designed for retail executives, Retail TouchPoints is known for its in-depth market research specific to the retail industry at large. Retail TouchPoints offers a free subscription-based newsletter that retailers big and small can learn from.

Shift Your Shopping, ShiftYourShopping.org Shift Your Shopping works with organizations that include the American Independent Business Alliance (AMIBA), the Business Alliance for Local Living Economies (BALLE), Causetown, and Kevin Bacon's SixDegrees.org to promote local and independent shopping. Although the message is targeted at consumers, the platform encourages retailers to get involved.

Shipwire, Shipwire.com For retailers who need more space to store inventory beyond their storefronts, Shipwire is a fantastic resource. The company offers storage, shipping, and management of inventory—helping retailers save time and costs and avoid unnecessary and complex shipping issues.

Shopify, Shopify.com Shopify allows retailers to easily create and manage an online store. Merchants can choose from over 100 professional templates that can be customized to their unique stores, also offering an easy-to-use back-end system for retail management. Shopify also provides educational resources on its website for retailers to learn from.

Shop Indie Retail, ShopIndieRetail.com This is an online directory of independent retail stores across the United States, highlighting their uniqueness and sharing contact details with customers.

ShopKeep POS, ShopKeep.com ShopKeep POS is a simple, easy-to-use point-of-sale system that is ideal for independent retailers and service-based businesses such as coffee shops. The cloud-based POS system helps retailers track sales, manage inventory, print or e-mail receipts, and more.

Shop Small, ShopSmall.com Shop Small was founded in 2010 by American Express and has since evolved to be a nationally recognized movement that supports small-business owners. The Saturday following Thanksgiving is officially recognized as Shop Small Saturday, and through the Shop Small network, retailers can gain a variety of tools and resources to help strengthen their store presence.

Sierra Pacific Crafts, SPC.us Sierra Pacific Crafts is a member-owned cooperative that works to create and sustain a vibrant community of family-owned retailers in creative industries through cooperative strategies in sharing, education, merchandising, marketing, operations, and more.

SnapRetail, SnapRetail.com SnapRetail is the only company to exclusively support independent retailers with online marketing that ranges from prewritten social media posts to professionally designed and prewritten e-mails, a drag-and-drop calendar, a library of images to use, and more.

Soldsie, Soldsie.com Soldsie software helps retailers to import their existing web store on to Facebook. The tools can help you promote products via Facebook and ultimately allow customers to make purchases directly from Facebook.

Square, SquareUp.com Square allows merchants to conveniently swipe credit cards via mobile devices and iPads with their Square Card reader. The company also offers other services and software to help merchants better manage their retail stores while also being compatible with a variety of POS providers.

STOPfakes, Stopfakes.gov STOPfakes is a one-stop shop for U.S. government resources and tools on intellectual property rights (IPRs). It assists and educates small and medium-sized enterprises (SMEs), consumers, government officials, and the general public about IPRs.

Store Specialty Services, SpecialtyStoreServices.com Discover a wide variety of store fixtures, store displays, and other related products. This online warehouse allows you to conveniently shop for your store.

Tarsus Group, tarsus.com Tarsus Group represents a number of trade shows and publications, including the Off-Price Show held in New York and Las Vegas annually.

TopTenWholesale, TopTenWholesale.com This is a vertical search engine that connects buyers of general merchandise wholesale products to manufacturers, importers, distributors, auctioneers, independent retailers, flea marketers, drop shippers, and any reseller of new and closeouts merchandise.

Trademarks The Spot, TMTheSpot.com Trademarks The Spot helps retailers and other business owners to take the necessary steps to protect their businesses. The legal team offers federal and state trademark searches, filing, monitoring, and more—often more affordable than other attorney rates.

Trade Show Exhibitors Association, TSEA.org This association provides knowledge to management and marketing professionals who promote and sell products through face-to-face marketing. This is a great resource for finding trade shows.

Tripar International, Tripar.com Beautifully showcase your products and inspire your customers with Tripar's boutique selection of fixtures, displays, tabletop stands, accessories, and more. The company's products are known to stand out among boutique retailers and help drive sales through displays.

United States Patent and Trademark Office, http://www.uspto.gov The U.S. Patent and Trademark Office (USPTO) registers trademarks and protects intellectual property (IP) for U.S. entrepreneurs and innovators worldwide.

U.S. Small Business Administration, SBA.gov The SBA has resources and information for starting and managing businesses, getting loans and grants, registering for government contracting, and receiving business counseling and training. In addition, the SBA supports regional Small Business Development Centers often adjacent to college or university campuses for more hands-on support.

Vend, VendHQ.com Vend is a POS, inventory, and customer-loyalty software that helps retailers manage and grow their businesses. The easy-to-use software is iPad-based and ideal for retailers in a diverse range of industries, including apparel, fashion, sports, health and beauty, food and drink, tourism, home goods, and more.

Vine, Vine.com Vine allows merchants to incorporate videos into their online messaging. This app is easy to use and can be used via social media, e-mail marketing, and other online efforts to help communicate details about your store or business.

Wishpond, Wishpond.com Wishpond is an app that makes it easy to run a group offer or social media contest to drive sales and traffic to a website or store with coupons and other special offers via Facebook, Twitter, Pinterest, your website, and mobile devices.

WholesaleCrafts.com, WholesaleCrafts.com Retailers can discover over a 1,000 American and Canadian wholesale artists on this online virtual marketplace. Buyers must be qualified retailers and, once approved, may enroll for free.

Wholesale Minded, RetailMinded.com/Wholesale-minded-magazine *Wholesale Minded Magazine* is a free digital publication from Retail Minded that shares expert insight, practical solutions, educational support, specifically to independent wholesalers, new-to-market vendors, and retailers who work with them.

APPENDIX B

Common Retail Terms and Definitions

I N THIS appendix we have provided a list of common retail terms to help support you in your overall understanding of the retail business at large. We'll also address common wholesale terms in an effort for you to best manage your supplier communication. Although retail includes many additional terms, this list is intended to support the most common words used in the retail industry.

We'd like to also thank Via Trading for its support in supplying many of the terms identified herein, and we encourage you to visit Via Trading's expansive glossary for additional retail and wholesale terminology at http://www.viatrading.com/wholesale/456/Glossary-of-Terms.html.

Acceptance   The act of a drawee acknowledging in writing on the face of a draft, payable at a fixed or determinable future date, that he or she will pay the draft at maturity.

Acceptance draft   A sight draft, documents against acceptance. See *Documents against acceptance.*

Airway bill   The carrying agreement between shipper and air carrier, which is obtained from the airline used to ship the goods.

All-risks clause   An insurance provision that provides additional coverage to an open cargo policy, usually for an additional premium. Contrary to its name, the clause does not protect against all risks. The more common perils it does cover are theft, pilferage, nondelivery, freshwater damage, contact with other cargo, breakage, and leakage. Inherent vice, loss of market, and losses caused by delay are not covered.

As-is   Refers to the selling conditions of certain merchandise. The buyer typically assumes all risks in purchasing such goods, and the merchandise is sold with no guarantees or returns.

ATA carnet   Customs document that enables one to carry or send goods temporarily into certain foreign countries without paying duties or posting bonds.

Authority to pay   A document comparable with a revocable letter of credit but under whose terms the authority to pay the seller stems from the buyer rather than from a bank.

B2B trade platforms   B2B trade platforms are business-to-business vertical search engines that connect buyers and sellers in global and domestic trade. These online marketplaces provide tools that are necessary to facilitate communication between retailers/resellers and wholesalers/manufacturers.

Balance of trade   The balance between a country's exports and imports.

Beneficiary   The person in whose favor a letter of credit is issued or a draft is drawn.

Big-box stores   Big-box stores are stand-alone retailers that carry assorted merchandise. An example would be Macy's or Target. Big-box stores also may be categorized as department stores, discount stores, or warehouse stores depending on the store itself.

Bill of exchange   See *Draft*.

Bill of lading   A document that provides the terms of the contract between the shipper and the transportation company to move freight between stated points at a specified charge.

Bonded warehouse   A building authorized by customs authorities for the storage of goods without payment of duties until removal.

Boutique   Refers to small shops or stores that are independently owned and often sell a product assortment that is not duplicated exactly in any other store.

Buy local (also referred to as Shop local)   A term used to identify the importance of shopping at local businesses, often used to communicate to consumers in an effort to strengthen local economic importance and small-business value.

Buying agent   An agent who buys in this country for foreign importers, especially for such large foreign users as mines, railroads, governments, and public utilities. Synonymous with *purchasing agent*.

Capital   The wealth, whether in money or property, owned by a business or individual.

Cash and carry   A form of wholesale that sells products on the spot, usually with cash only, to a purchaser who is then able to self-carry the products themselves without having to wait for any time between purchasing and delivery.

Cash wrap [also referred to as point-of-sale (POS) Area] The place where a consumer goes to purchase products or services within a store, often the same area in which purchases are wrapped in bags for customers.

Carrier   A transportation line that hauls cargo.

Case packs   Generally refers to items packed in a small case, typically in quantities of 6, 12, 24, or 100. Goods such as cosmetics, clothing, accessories, and jewelry are often sold in case packs, representing a predetermined item count.

Certificate of free sale   A certificate, required by some foreign governments, stating that the goods for export (if products are under the jurisdiction of the U.S. Federal Food and Drug Administration) are acceptable for sale in the United States; that is, that the products are sold freely, without restriction. The Food and Drug Administration (FDA) will issue shippers a letter of comment to satisfy foreign requests or regulations.

Certificate of inspection   A document in which certification is made as to the good condition of the merchandise immediately prior to shipment. The buyer usually designates the inspecting organization, which is typically an independent inspection firm or government body.

Certificate of manufacture A statement by a producer, sometimes notarized, that certifies that manufacturing has been completed and that the goods are at the disposal of the buyer.

Certificate of origin A document in which certification is made as to the country of origin of the merchandise.

C&F Cost and freight. Same as CIF, except that insurance is covered by the buyer.

CFR Cost and freight indicates that the seller will deliver the goods to the buyer and apply actual cost of freight to the buyers.

Chamber of Commerce An association of businesspeople whose purpose is to promote commercial and industrial interests in the community.

CIF Cost, insurance, and freight. A pricing term under which the seller pays all expenses involved in the placing of merchandise on board a carrier and in addition prepays the freight and insures the goods (an automatic condition of the contract) to an agreed-on destination.

Clean bill of lading A bill of lading signed by the transportation company indicating that the shipment has been received in good condition with no irregularities in the packing or general condition of all or any part of the shipment.

Closeout Selling the entire lot of remaining merchandise usually through a sale at reduced prices.

Collection The procedure involved in a bank's collecting money for a seller against a draft drawn on a buyer abroad, usually through a correspondent bank.

COD   Cash on delivery. If your goods are delivered according to COD terms, you must pay cash for them. COD is common for retailers when credit is tight.

Collection papers   The documents submitted, usually with a draft or against a letter of credit, for payment of an export shipment.

Commercial invoice   A trade invoice that identifies charges applied from a purchase or service.

Consignee   The person, firm, or representative to whom a seller or shipper sends merchandise and who, on presentation of the necessary documents, is recognized as the owner of the merchandise for the purpose of the payment of customs duties. This term is also used as applying to one to whom goods are shipped, usually at the shipper's risk, when an outright sale has not been made. See *Consignment*.

Consignment   A term pertaining to merchandise that has not been purchased, under an agreement by which the consignee is obligated to sell the goods for the account of the consignor and to remit proceeds as goods are sold.

Consumers   The final purchaser, or end user, of any product or service. In retail specifically, consumers are often referred to as customers.

Correspondent bank   A bank that is a depository for another bank, accepting deposits and collecting items for its bank depositor.

Country of origin   The country in which a product or commodity is manufactured or produced.

Credit risk insurance   A form of insurance that protects the seller against loss due to default on the part of the buyer.

Customer return   Item that has been purchased by a customer and then returned to the store (or online store) for any number of reasons.

Customs   The agency or procedure for collecting duties imposed by a country on imports or exports.

D/A   See *Documents against acceptance.*

Dead stock   Inventory in a store that has never been purchased by a consumer and reflects products from past seasons. Despite multiple attempts to sell it, this stock does not sell. Dead stock is often a result of inexperienced buying, including lack of knowledge of the customer base.

Defective   Defective condition refers to items that have been put through a testing process and have been deemed defective or not working. Items may be visually defective or incomplete or be missing parts. Items also may be brand new but with a major quality-control flaw, making them defective.

Demographics   Identifies population in groups based on age, gender, income, occupation, education, religion, race, family size, family lifestyle, and more. Government studies often provide demographic information and select retail groups or organizations specific to their niche retail category.

Direct shipment   Refers to items that are shipped to the customer directly from a store's facility.

Discount   A reduction in the price of an item. Discounts will vary in amount and purpose.

Displays   Represents the visual appearance of a store environment, often referring to specific areas of a store—such as a window display, table display, or point-of-sale (POS) display.

Discrepancy, letter of credit   When documents presented do not conform to the terms of the letter of credit, it is referred to as a *discrepancy.*

Distributor   A firm that sells directly for a manufacturer, usually on an exclusive basis for a specified territory, and that maintains an inventory on hand.

Documents against acceptance (D/A)   A type of payment for goods in which the documents transferring title to the goods are not given to the buyer until he or she has accepted the draft issued against him or her.

Documents against payment (D/P)   A type of payment for goods in which the documents transferring title to the goods are not given to the buyer until he or she has paid the value of a draft issued against him or her.

Domestic International Sales Corporation (DISC)   An export sales corporation set up by a U.S. company under U.S government authorization to promote exports from the United States by giving the exporter economic advantages not available outside such authorization.

D/P   See *Documents against payment.*

Draft (also known as bill of exchange)   A written order for a certain sum of money to be transferred on a certain date from the person who owes the money or who agrees to make the payment (the drawee) to the creditor to whom the money is owed (the drawer of the draft).

Drawee   One on whom a draft is drawn and who owes the stated amount. See *Draft.*

Drawer   One who draws a draft and receives payment. See *Draft.*

Drop shipping   An order that is placed with a vendor and shipped directly to the end consumer. (Brokers deal with drop shippers when they do not want to touch or warehouse the merchandise. They receive orders from their customers and then place a drop-ship order with a vendor, who then ships the merchandise directly to the broker's customer.) Drop-ship orders are typically shipped blind, meaning with no trace of the vendor's name or address, to protect the broker.

Duty   The tax imposed by a government on merchandise imported from another country.

E-mail blast   An e-mail sent to a large group of people at once.

EMC   An export management company.

Employee turnover   The ratio between the number of employees who had to be replaced and the number of average employees in a given period of time. For example, if you have an average of six employees in a year and three people had to be replaced because they quit that year, your turnover would be 50 percent. *Turnover* is the opposite of *retention*.

ETC   An export trading company.

Exchange permit   A government permit sometimes required of an importer to enable him or her to convert his or her own country's currency into a foreign currency with which to pay a seller in another country.

Exchange regulations/restrictions   Restrictions imposed by an importing country to protect its foreign-exchange reserves. See *Exchange permit*.

Excise tax   A domestic tax assessed on the manufacture, sale, or use of a commodity within a country. Usually refundable if the product is exported.

Expiration date   The final date on which the presentation of documents and drawing of drafts under a letter of credit may be made.

Export   To send goods to a foreign country or overseas territory.

Export broker   One who brings together the exporter and importer for a fee and then withdraws from the transaction.

EXW (ex works)   Indicates that the buyer is responsible for cargo when it's available at the seller's factory.

Factoring company (also referred to as a factor)   A business organization that lends money on accounts receivable or buys and collects accounts receivable. *Factors* make funds available to retailers.

FCA (free carrier at)   Indicates that the seller delivers the goods to the named place free of any transportation cost, having cleared the cargo for export. The seller accepts transportation costs, risks, and responsibilities until the cargo is handed over at the named place.

Focus group   A group of people (e.g., your customers) brought together to give their opinions on a particular issue or product, often for the purpose of market research or inventory strategies; usually no more than 10 to 12 people.

General license (export)   Government authorization to export without specific documentary approval.

Gross weight   Total weight of goods, packing, and container, ready for shipment.

Handling charges   The forwarder's fee to the shipping client.

Import   To bring merchandise into a country from another country or overseas territory.

Import license   A government document that permits the importation of a product or material into a country where such licenses are necessary.

Inco terms   Indicate whether the buyer or the seller carries the risk, responsibility, liability, or costs at specific points during a transaction.

Inconvertibility   The inability to exchange the currency of one country for the currency of another.

Insurance certificate   A document issued by an insurance company, usually to order of shipper, under a marine policy and in cover of a particular shipment of merchandise.

Internship   Any program, formal or informal, that provides practical experience for beginners in an occupation or profession. Retailers often seek to hire interns to help in specific areas of their businesses, such as visual merchandising or social media, as a way to gain store support that they may not normally have access to otherwise.

Invoice   A document that identifies charges applied from a purchase or service. See *Commercial invoice.*

Irrevocable   Applied to letters of credit. An irrevocable letter of credit is one that cannot be altered or canceled once it has been negotiated between the buyer and his or her bank.

Joint venture   A commercial or industrial enterprise in which principals of one company share control and ownership with principals of another company.

Kiosk   A free-standing structure used in a public place, such as a mall, that is designed to support a product or service to be sold to consumers. It is also used for interactive opportunities and may be on a short-term basis, such as when used during a festival.

L/C   See *Letter of credit.*

Legal weight   The weight of goods plus any immediate wrappings that are sold along with the goods, for example, the weight of a tin can together with its contents. See *Net weight.*

Letter of credit (L/C) (commercial)   A document issued by a bank at a buyer's request in favor of a seller, promising to pay an agreed amount of money on receipt by the bank of certain documents within a specified time.

Licensing   The grant of technical assistance and service and/or the use of proprietary rights, such as a trademark or patent, in return for royalty payments.

Line of credit   Same as a credit limit; the maximum amount of credit that a store is authorized to use by a bank or other lender.

Line sheet   A document that collectively represents products from a specific brand or vendor, sharing details on product prices—including wholesale and retail—as well as product availability, shipping terms, contents of products, and more.

Look book   A book that is similar to a portfolio, but it represents a product line rather than providing visual samples of one's work history. The purpose of a look book is to provide a "story," "feeling," or "inspirational overview" of the product assortment through photographs of the products being sold.

Markdown   A devaluation of a product based on its inability to be sold at the original planned selling price.

Markup   Increase in the price of a product or service to create a profit margin for the business.

Manufactured suggested retail price (MSRP; also recognized as retail value)   The value and suggested retail price a vendor, supplier, or wholesaler identifies a product to be sold at.

Manufacturer   Refers to handmade or machine-constructed products that begin as raw materials and are completed into finished goods that are for use or sale to wholesalers as well as retailers.

Master case   100 percent brand-new factory-sealed merchandise, still in its original packaging.

Maturity date   The date on which a draft or acceptance becomes due for payment.

MOQ (minimum order quantity)   A MOQ is the smallest quantity of a product that a supplier requires you to buy in a single purchase.

Net weight   The weight of the goods alone without any immediate wrappings, for example, the weight of the contents of a tin can without the weight of the can.

Online marketplace   Refers to a type of e-commerce website where product is available to be sourced for a retail store. Typically, transactions are processed by this online marketplace and then delivered and fulfilled by the participating suppliers (wholesalers).

Open to buy (OTB)   Refers to the portion of a retail budget available to spend on inventory at any given time. Used to identify how much money is available to place orders for store product.

Operating expenses   The expenses involved in running a business.

Packing list   A list that shows the number and kinds of packages being shipped; totals of gross, legal, and net weights of the packages; and marks and numbers on the packages. The list may be requested by a retailer or supplied voluntarily by a vendor or supplier.

Point of sale (POS)   Traditionally speaking, POS represents the place where an actual transaction is completed. In modern retail, POS often refers to software that processes a transaction in exchange for goods or services sold.

Pop-up shop   The act of opening a short-term storefront, often applying to only one day, although it may apply to a weekend or as long as a month.

Product sourcing   The act of finding products from wholesalers or manufacturers to resell through a business.

Pro forma invoice   An invoice forwarded by the seller of goods prior to shipment to advise the buyer of the weight and value of the goods.

Psychographics   Identifies lifestyles and stages that appear to influence consumer shopping decisions. Includes activities, beliefs, habits, opinions, and more, of customers.

Quota   The total quantity of a product or commodity that may be imported into a country without restriction or the penalty of additional duties or taxes.

Quotation   An offer to sell goods at a stated price and under stated terms.

Rate of exchange   The basis on which money of one country will be exchanged for that of another. Rates of exchange are established and quoted for foreign currencies on the basis of the demand, supply, and stability of the individual currencies. See *Exchange*.

Retail   The business of selling services or products that ultimately will be sold to consumers, the end users of the products or services purchased.

Retail supply chain   A product is created at a manufacturer, is sold to a wholesaler, and then is sold again to a retailer, who ultimately sells the product to the final purchaser, the consumer.

Retail value [also recognized as manufactured suggested retail price (MSRP)]   The value of an item as suggested by a supplier or vendor for retailers to sell the product at retail.

Retailer   A fixed location, including storefronts, the Internet, kiosks, and pop-up shops, that sell products or services to consumers. In addition, the term *retailer* can be applied to the person who owns a retail store.

Revocable   Applied to letters of credit. A revocable letter of credit is one that can be altered or canceled by the buyer after he or she has opened it through his or her bank.

RFQ (also referred to as RFP)   Request for quotation or request for proposal. A business process that invites suppliers to bid on specific products or services. It allows suppliers to provide quotations for their goods and services to retailers and/or distributors.

Royalty payment   The share of the product or profit paid by a licensee to his or her licenser. See *Licensing*.

Sales representative   A representative of a company, either contract-based or as an employee of a particularly company, who represents a product being sold. Typically, sales representatives will work for vendors attempting to secure their products within retail stores.

Seasonal goods   Goods that are heavy in merchandise for a particular season, such as Halloween, Easter, Christmas, and so on.

Sell-through   The ratio between the quantity of goods sold by a retailer and the quantity originally delivered to the wholesaler; number of pieces sold divided by number of original pieces delivered. If you sell five of eight pairs of pants, your *sell-through* is 62.5 percent.

Shipper's export declaration   A form required by the U.S. Treasury Department and completed by a shipper showing the value, weight, consignee, destination, and so on, of export shipments as well as a Schedule B identification number.

Shipping documents   Commercial invoices, bills of lading, insurance certificates, consular invoices, and related documents.

Stocking distributor   A distributor who maintains an inventory of goods of a manufacturer.

Supplier   May refer to manufacturer, distributor, wholesaler, or vendor. Collectively represents all these product professionals.

Sustainable   If something is *sustainable*, it does not harm the environment or deplete natural resources. In retailing, it often refers to *sustainable design*, whether that be in building design or product design.

Tare weight   The weight of packing and containers without the goods to be shipped.

Tariff A schedule or system of duties imposed by a government on goods imported or exported; the rate of duty imposed in a tariff.

Tenor The time fixed or allowed for payment, as in "the tenor of a draft."

Time draft A draft drawn to mature at a certain fixed time after presentation or acceptance.

Trade shows Trade shows are organized events that cater to a specific industry and introduce buyers and sellers. Traditionally, trade shows are closed to the public and are only accessible to registered buyers and members of the retail trade.

Validated license A government document authorizing the export of commodities within the limitations set forth in the document.

Visa A signature of formal approval on a document. Obtained from consulates.

Visual merchandising The art of using effective design and merchandising ideas that will enhance the shopping experience of a store as well as increase sales and foot traffic.

Wholesale The selling of goods through a business-to-business transaction of large quantities to retailers.

Wholesaler An individual or company that sells a product or service to a retailer and does not sell this product or service directly to consumers.

Notes

1: Standing Out among Other Retailers

1. Kimberly Efseaff, owner and designer, Bon Bijoux Girly Boutique. Interview by Nicole Reyhle, December 14, 2013.

2: Stepping Outside Your Comfort Zone

1. Macquenzi Farquer, owner, Lockport, Astoria, New York. Interview by Nicole Reyhle, October 15, 2013.

2. Ibid.

3. Shari Ralish, owner, Peaceful Parlour. Interview by Nicole Reyhle, November 11, 2013.

4. Joe Abraham, author of *Entrepreneurial DNA*. Interview by Nicole Reyhle, December 12, 2013, Geneva, Illinois.

3: Leaning on Outside Organizations

1. Ellen Divita, economic development director, City of Geneva. Interview by Nicole Reyhle, November 3, 2013, Geneva, Illinois.

2. Ibid.

3. Harriet Parker, manager, Aurora, Illinois–based Small Business Development Center. Interview by Nicole Reyhle, October 21, 2013, Geneva, Illinois.

4. Andy Ellen, president and general counsel, North Carolina Retail Merchants Association. Interview by Nicole Reyhle via e-mail, October 28, 2013.

5. Ibid.

6. Curtis Picard, executive director, Retail Association of Maine. Interview by Nicole Reyhle, October 29, 2013.

7. Ibid.

8. Ibid.

9. Jama Rice, executive director and CEO of Museum Store Association, interview by Nicole Reyhle via e-mail, November 6, 2013.

10. Missy Brozek, vice president and creative director, Crafter's Home. Interview by Nicole Reyhle, January 1, 2014.

4: Identifying Your Unique Store Story

1. Angela Gianfrancesco, owner, Stella Blue Designs. Interview by Nicole Reyhle, October 18, 2013, Chicago, Illinois.

2. Ibid.

3. Ibid.

4. Kirt Manecke, author and customer-service expert. Interview by Nicole Reyhle, November 2013.

5: Sourcing Products Through Trade Shows and the Internet

1. Megy Karydes, owner, Karydes Consulting. Interview by Nicole Reyhle, January 2, 2014, Chicago, Illinois.

2. Ibid.

3. Camille Candella, group marketing manager, Emerald Expositions. Interview by Nicole Reyhle, December 5, 2013.

4. Jonathan Prescott, senior business manager, JP Communications, Inc. Interview by Nicole Reyhle, December 14, 2013.

6: Buying for Customer versus Yourself

1. Cathy Wagner, CEO, RetailMAVENS. Interview by Nicole Reyhle, November 11, 2013, Geneva, Illinois.

2. Dr. Gary Edwards, chief customer officer, Mindshare Technologies. Originally shared via RetailMinded.com in an article published by Retail Minded, January 2014.

3. Tom Konopacki, owner, Anastazia. Interview by Nicole Reyhle, December 2013, Geneva, Illinois.

4. Vaughan Rowsell, CEO, Vend. Interview by Nicole Reyhle, December 29, 2013.

5. Ibid.

6. Ibid.

7. Dr. Gary Edwards, chief customer officer, Mindshare Technologies. Originally shared via RetailMinded.com in an article published by Retail Minded, January 2014.

8. Cathy Wagner, CEO, RetailMAVENS. Interview by Nicole Reyhle, December 9, 2013, Geneva, Illinois.

9. Ibid.

10. Ibid.

7: Selling Your Products

1. Michael Amato, president and CEO, Cimarron, Inc.

2. Angela Gianfrancesco, owner, Stella Blue Designs. Interview by Nicole Reyhle, October 18, 2013, Chicago, Illinois.

3. Ibid.

4. Rich Kizer and Georganne Bender, Kizer & Bender Speaking. Interview by Nicole Reyhle, November 5, 2013, St. Charles, Illinois.

5. Kerry Bannigan, cofounder, Nolcha Fashion Week, New York. Interview by Nicole Reyhle, November 25, 2013, New York City.

6. Cathy Wagner, CEO, RetailMAVENS. Interview by Nicole Reyhle, November 1, 2013, Geneva, Illinois.

7. Rich Kizer and Georganne Bender, Kizer & Bender Speaking. Interview by Nicole Reyhle, November 5, 2013, St. Charles, Illinois.

8. Vaughan Rowsell, CEO, Vend. Interview by Nicole Reyhle, December 30, 2013.

9. Ibid.

10. Jason Richelson, founder and CEO, ShopKeep POS. Interview by Nicole Reyhle, November 25, 2013, New York, New York.

8: Applying Press and Marketing to Your Business

1. Cynthia Sutton, owner, Silver Barn retail store. Interview by Nicole Reyhle, October 16, 2013, Columbus, Texas.

2. Ibid.

3. Suzy Teele, COO, SnapRetail.com. Interview by Nicole Reyhle, November 2, 2013.

4. Ibid.

5. Ibid.

6. Jessica Moretti, marketing communications manager, SnapRetail .com. Interview by Nicole Reyhle, December 10, 2013.

7. Courtney Rodgers, cofounder, Boutique Window. Interview by Nicole Reyhle, November 27, 2013.

8. Cynthia Sutton, owner, Silver Barn retail store. Interview by Nicole Reyhle, October 16, 2013, Columbus, Texas.

9: Making Your Presence Online

1. Don Davis, editor-in-chief, *Internet Retailer Magazine*. Interview by Nicole Reyhle, November 2013, Chicago, Illinois.

2. Harley Finkelstein, chief platform officer, Shopify.com. Interview by Nicole Reyhle in October 2013.

3. Ibid.

4. Courtney Rodgers, cofounder, Boutique Window. Interview by Nicole Reyhle, November 27, 2014.

5. Ibid.

6. Don Davis, editor in chief of Internet Retailer Magazine. Interviewed by Nicole Reyhle, November 2013, Chicago, Illinois.

7. Ibid.

8. Forrester Research released a report titled "U.S. Cross Channel Retail Forecast" on October 29, 2013 that identified this finding, which can be found at forrester.com.

9. Don Davis, editor-in-chief, *Internet Retailer Magazine.* Interview by Nicole Reyhle, November 2013, Chicago, Illinois.

10. Ibid.

11. Skip McGrath, publisher, SkipMcGrath.com. Interview by Nicole Reyhle, December 6, 2013.

12. Suzy Teele, COO, SnapRetail. Interview by Nicole Reyhle, November 25, 2013.

13. Ibid.

14. Ed Cleary, publisher, Retail TouchPoints. Interview by Nicole Reyhle, November 25, 2013.

15. Rich Kizer and Georganne Bender, Kizer & Bender Speaking. Interview by Nicole Reyhle, November 2013, St. Charles, Illinois.

16. Ibid.

17. Suzy Teele, COO, SnapRetail. Interview by Nicole Reyhle, November 25, 2013.

18. Ella Wirtz, cofounder, Boutique Window. Interview by Nicole Reyhle, November 27, 2013.

10: Taking Part in Shop-Local Initiatives

1. Mackenzi Farquer, owner, Lockport, Astoria, New York. Interview by Nicole Reyhle, New York City, October 16, 2013.

2. Jeff Milchen, codirector, AMIBA. Interview by Nicole Reyhle, November 23, 2013.

3. Ibid.

4. Ibid.

5. Ibid.

6. Mitchen. Identified in company overview on AMBIA.net, November 2013.

7. Ibid.

8. Identified in a report released by the National Federation of Independent Businesses and American Express Research, December 2013.

9. Susan Sobbott, president, American Express OPEN, shared in a press release statement released July 2013.

10. Ibid.

11. Amy Knebel, Washington DC-based customer. Interview by Nicole Reyhle, December 6, 2013.

12. Dan McCabe, CEO, Causetown.org. Interview by Nicole Reyhle, December 9, 2013.

11: A Crystal Ball for Independent Retailers

1. Kimberly Efseaff, Bon Bijoux Girly Boutique, Del Mar, California. Interview by Nicole Reyhle, December 28, 2013.

2. Angela Gianfrancesco, owner, Stella Blue Designs. Interview by Nicole Reyhle, October 18, 2013, Chicago, Illinois.

3. Jason Richelson, founder and CEO, ShopKeep POS. Interview by Nicole Reyhle, November 25, 2013.

4. Vaughan Rowsell, CEO, Vend. Interview by Nicole Reyhle, December 28, 2013.

5. Camille Candella, group marketing manager, Emerald Expositions. Interview by Nicole Reyhle, December 5, 2013.

6. Bill McNulty, publisher, Sumner Communications, Inc.. Interview by Nicole Reyhle, December 28, 2013.

7. Angela Gianfrancesco, owner of Stella Blue Designs. Interview by Nicole Reyhle, October 18, 2013, Chicago, Illinois.

8. Curtis Kroeker, BizBuySell.com and BizQuest.com. Interview by Nicole Reyhle, November 18, 2013.

Index

70-20-10 rule, in social media, 170

Abraham, Joe, 9, 14
Accessories Resource Team (ART), 32, 206
Action Guides, 5
Adidas, xv–xvi
Advanstar, 44, 205
Advisory boards, customer-based, 95–97
Alabama Retail Association, 34
Amato, Michael, 108
Amazon, 153, 164, 165
America's Mart, 73
American Apparel & Footwear Association, 32, 206
American Express, 183, 215–216
American Independent Business Alliance (AMIBA), 146, 178–182, 185, 206, 214
American Specialty Toy Retailing Association (ASTRA), 32
Anastazia, 98
Android, 190
Apple, Inc., 39, 191
Apps, 194. *See also* iPods
Arizona Retailers Association, 34
Arkansas Grocers and Retail Merchants Assoc., 34
Aroma, 130
ART Home Furnishings Network, 32, 206

ASD Trade Show, xviii, 17, 42, 43, 62, 66, 70, 71, 74, 206, 210
Associated Oregon Industries Retail Council, 34
Association of Small Business Development Centers, 206

Bacon, Kevin, 215
BALLE calculators, 182
Bandholz, Eric, 156
Bank of America, 207
Bannigan, Kerry, xviii, 116
Barneys, 191
BeALocalist.org., 207
Beardbrand, 156, 158
Beckham, David, xvi
Beetailer, 172, 207
Bender, Georganne, 112, 118, 169, 170, 213
Benefits of organizations, 29
Berg, Bob, 78
Best Buy, 165
Big-box competition, 10–12
Bing, 80
BizBuySell, 197, 200, 207
BizQuest, 197
Blog.trade.gove, 69
Blogging, xvi–xvii
Bon Bijoux Girly Boutique, 189
Bosi DNA, 207
Boutique Vision, 208

Boutique Window, 144, 146, 159, 171, 172, 202, 207
Branding, 139
Brozek, Missy, 28
Buehler, Jef, 21
Builder entrepreneurs, 9
Bureau of Labor Statistics, 208
Business Alliance for Local Living Economies (BALLE), 181–182, 185, 207, 214–215
Business cards, 76
Business insurance, 30
Business-to-Business (B2B) sourcing platforms, 80–85
BusinessUSA, 208
Buy-local campaigns, 5, 178–182
Buyers, xiv
Buyers' guides, 29
Buying, 89–105
Buying districts, wholesale, 73

Calculators, BALLE, 182
Calendar for store, 109–111
California Retailers Association, 34
Call to action (CTA) in marketing message, 142
Candella, Camille, 76, 194
Cardlytics, 201, 208
CardPrinting.us, 48
Causetown.org, 185–186, 208, 215
CES trade show, 43, 71
Chambers of Commerce, 4, 22–23, 33
Chanel, Coco, 3
Charity events, 134, 185–186
Chasalla, xiii
Checkout procedures, 46–47
Children's Club trade show, 43
Choosing/selecting your inventory, 41–42
Churchill, Winston, 177
Cimarron, 108
City of Geneva, Illinois, 22
CitySearch.com, 97
Claire's Boutique, 12
Cleary, Ed, 167, 169
Cloud computing, 191, 192
Cloud-based point-of-sale (POS), 210
Coastal.com, 165
Colorado Retail Council, 34

Comfort zone expansion, 9–20
Community-based supports, 4–5, 22–37
Company contact info, online store, 161
Company philosophy, 56
Competition, 16
  big-box stores as, 10–12
  identifying, 10–12
  learning from, 16
Conferences, 29, 33
Connecticut Retail Merchants Association, 34
Constant Contact, 143
Consumer Electronics Show, 71
Contact information, for store, 56, 161
Content marketing, 175–176
Content of marketing message, 142
Council of State Retail Associations (CSRA), 209
Couture trade show, 43
Craft & Hobby Association, 32, 209
Craft and Hobby Retailers, 32
Crafters' Home, xviii, 28, 209
Crain's Chicago Business, xvii
Creating an online store, 155–163
Credit card sales, 201, 216
Cross-merchandising techniques, 122
Cuban, Mark, 153
Customer care/customer service, 20, 44, 45, 47–48, 54, 57, 138, 194–197
  customer feedback and, 95–97, 104
  customer resource management (CRS) in, 192
  disputes in, 49–50
  importance of, 194–197
  inviting customers to events in, 114–115
  online store, 163
  review sites and, 97
Customer disputes, 49–50
Customer feedback, 95–97, 104
Customer resource management (CRS), 192
Customers
  identifying, 47
  targeting, 7, 15, 163
  understanding habits of, 15, 19–20
Customs regulations, 65

Daily store routines, 20
Dallas Market Center, The, 73

Dallas Mavericks, 153
Dance Retailer News, xvii
Data sources, 15
Davis, Don, 154, 158, 162
Delaware Retail Council, Inc., 35
DeMaria, Jennifer, 166
DHL, 65
Dick's Sporting Goods, xvi
Dillards, xiv
Discounted merchandise, 121–122
Displays, display hardware, 117–123, 150
    cross-merchandising techniques in,
        122
    immediate-right zone in, 120
    lighting and, 118
    point of sale (POS) areas and, 121
    sale section in, 121–122
    staples vs. statements in, 122–123
    store stoppers as, 120–121
    store windows as, 119
Diversifying your inventory, 11–13
Divita, Ellen, 22
Do It In Person, 172, 209
Dress code, 58
Drucker, Peter, 189

E-commerce, 153
    statistics on, 145
E-mail marketing, 140, 141–144
eBay, 164, 165
Educational opportunities at trade
    shows, 82
Edwards, Gary, 97, 102
Efseaff, Kimberly, 3–4, 189
Ellen, Andy, 25
Emerald Expositions, 44, 76, 194, 209
Emergency procedures, 58
Employee manuals, 58
Employees and staff, 7, 50–53. See also
    Operation procedures, 57
    employee manual for, 58
    employment practices, 56
    full vs. part–time, 18
    hiring, 51–53
    interviewing, 51–53
    managers as, hiring, 52–53
    termination of, 57
Employment practices, 56
Engaging the senses in selling, 128–131

ENT International, 205
Entrepreneurial DNA (Abraham), 9, 14
Entrepreneurs, 9
Etienne Aigner, xv
Events
    advance planning for, 114, 116–117
    expenses vs. sales generated by, 116
    in-store experience as centerpiece of,
        115–116
    introducing and managing, 108–117
    inviting customers to, 114–115
    marketing, 114
    planning dates for, 113
    regular scheduling of, 112
    store calendar for, 109–111
    tracking response to, 113–116
"Experience" of a store, 3. See also
    Engaging the senses

Fab.com, 165
Facebook, 47, 123, 144, 166, 171, 183, 201,
    207, 218
Farquer, Macquenzi, 10, 177
Fashion Footwear Association of New
    York (FFANY), 42
Federal Express, 65
Feedback from customers, 95–97, 104
Financing, 211
Finkelstein, Harley, 154
First impressions, in marketing, 142
Floral Retailers, 32
Florida Retail Federation, xviii, 35
Focus groups, 45
Footwear News magazine, xv
Forbes, xvii
Forrester Research, online shopping,
    159, 163
FourSquare, 123
Franco Sarto, xiv
Free shipping, online store, 162–163
Freight, 65
Fringe Sport, 156, 158
Future trends, 189–203

Gander Mountain, xvi
Garment district, New York, 73
Gates, Bill, 61, 89
Generational targeting, 7
Georgia Retail Association, 35

Gianfrancesco, Angela, 4–5, 41, 109, 196–197
Gift boxes/wrapping, 139
Gift certificates, 48
Gift Fair, NY, 43
Glamour magazine, xv
Global Shop, 210
GlobalSources.com, 81
Glossary of common retail terms, 219–235
Google, 80, 164
Google Glass, 201
Google Places, 201
Google+ in, 171
Gross margin, 93
Gross sales, 93
Group memberships, 7
Growing your business, 102–103

Habits of successful retailers, 14–19
Handheld/portable cash registers, 190–191, 194
Health insurance, 30
Hiring employees, 51–53
Hollis, Karen, 95
Home Furnishings Industry, 32

Idaho Retailers Association, 35
Ideation, 211
Illinois Retail Merchants Association, 35
Illinois Small business Development Center, 24
Immediate-right zone, 120
Importing merchandise, 65
Improvement District Programs of New Jersey, 21
Independent Jewelry Retailers and Vendors, 32
Independent Pet Retailers, 32
Independent Retailer Conference, xviii, 210
Independent Retailer Magazine, 210
IndiaMART.com, 81
Indiana Retail Council, 35
Industry publications, 31
Information sources, 15
InnoMark Communications, 208
Innovator entrepreneurs, 9
Instagram in, 171

Institute for Local Self-Reliance, 178, 185, 211
Insurance, 30
Intellectual property (IP), 217
Intellectual property rights (IPRs), 216
Internal Revenue Service (IRS), 211
International Business at the Sourcing, 78
International sourcing, 64, 66
International Trade Organization, 69
Internet, 61
sourcing through, 66
Internet Retailer Conference and Exhibition (IRCE), 162, 211
Internet Retailer Magazine, 154, 158, 164, 172, 210
Internet-based marketing, 139, 144–146
InternetRetailer.com, 162
Interviewing potential hires, 51–53
Introducing new items for sale, 108–117
Inventory management, xv, 19, 41–42, 138
choosing/selecting, 41–42
classification of items in, 90–91, 103–104
customer feedback to influence, 95–97, 104
displays, display hardware for, 117–123
diversifying in, 11–13
dollar value of, vs. units, 92
introducing new items in, 108–117
maintained markup (MMU), 94
open to buy (OTB) planning in, 93, 94
point of sale software for, 99–102
ranking performance of classes in, 104–105
retail math basics in, 90–95
stock-keeping unit (SKU) numbers in, 104
trade shows and, 41–44
turnover, 93
vendors and, 93
Inventory turnover, 93
iOS, 190
Iowa Retail Federation, 35
iPads, 123–126, 216
iPad Enclosures, 126, 210
iPad point-of-sale (POS), 123–126, 210
ISS trade show, 43

JCK trade show, 43
Jenny Boston, 166
Jobs, Steve, 39
JP Communications, Inc., xvii, 85

K. Hollis Jewelers, 95
Kabbage, 211
Kansas Chamber of Commerce, 35
Karydes Consulting, 63
Karydes, Megy, 63
Keeping it simple, in marketing
    message, 142
Keller, Alex, 156
Keller, Peter, 156
Kentucky Retail Federation, 35
Kizer & Bender Speaking, 112, 118, 169,
    170, 213
Kizer, Rich, 112, 118, 169, 170, 213
Knebel, Amy, 184
Konopacki, Tom, 98
Kroeker, Curtis, 197–200

Layout consistency, online store, 160
Learning, 16–17
Licensing Expo, 211–212
Licensing, 211–212
Lighting, 118
Local events, 40. *See also* Buy-local
    events
Local media, 16
Lockport, 10
Lord & Taylor, xiv
Louisiana Retailers Association, 35
Lucky magazine, xv

Macy's, xiv
Made-in-china.com, 81
MAGIC Market Week, 212
MAGIC trade show, 43, 62, 78, 205
Mail Chimp, 143
Main Street New Jersey, 21
Maintained markup (MMU), 94
Management One, 212
Managers, hiring, 52–53
Managing your business, 18
Manecke, Kirt, 54
Manufacturers.com, xvii, 62, 81, 212
Manufacturing.net, 69
Market research, 30, 45, 47, 95–97

Marketing, 16, 20, 40, 133
    branding and, 139
    charity events as, 134
    e-mail in, 140, 141–144
    events, 114
    gift boxes, bags, etc., 139
    importance of, 138
    Internet-based, 144–146
    online, 139
    resources and information on,
        146–148
    social media in, 140–141
Maryland Retailers Association, 35
Math, retail math basics, 90–95
Max Studio, xiii
Maynard, Kristin, 166
McCabe, Dane, 186
McGrath, Skip, 164, 165
McNulty, Bill, 195–196
Media, local, 16, 20
Merchandising, 57
Merchant solution benefits, 30–31
MFG.com, 81
Miami Merchandise Mart, The, 73
Michigan Retailers Association, 35
Midwest Market Days, 73
Milchen, Jeff, 178–182
Mindshare Technologies, 97
Minnesota Main Street, xviii
Minnesota Retailers Association, 35
Minority Business Development Agency
    (MBDA), 212
Mississippi Retail and Grocers
    Association, 35
Missouri Retailers Association, 35
Mobile commerce, 126–128
Modalyst, 81, 212
Montana Retail Association, 35
Moo.com, 147, 213
Moretti, Jessica, 142
Museum and Not–for–Profit Stores, 32
Museum Store Association, xviii, 27, 32
Museums & More, xvii
Music, 124, 129–130, 147

Nam.org, 69
National Federation of Independent
    Businesses, 183
National Hardware Show, 43, 71, 213

National Retail Federation, 48
Nebraska Retail Federation, 35
Net sales, 93
New Jersey Retail Merchants
    Association, 36
New Mexico Retail Association, 36
New York International Gift Fair, 43
New York wholesale/garment district, 73
NexPet, 32
Nielsen Expositions, 209
Nine West, xiv
Nolcha Events, 116
Nolcha Fashion Week/New York,
    xviii
Nordstrom, xiii, xiv, 44, 191
North Carolina Retail Merchants
    Association, 25, 36
North Dakota Retail Association, 36

Off–Price Show, 217
Ohio Council of Retail Merchants, 36
Online groups, 30
Online marketing. *See* Internet-based
    marketing
Online presence/online store, 7, 31,
    153–176, 201
    Amazon, eBay platforms for, 164, 165
    company contact info in, 161
    content marketing and, 175–176
    creating an online store for, 155–163
    customer care/customer service
        and, 163
    e-commerce and, 154–163
    Facebook as sales platform in, 166
    focus on your unique image in,
        158–159
    free shipping and, 162–163
    layout consistency in, 160
    payment options for, 161–162
    photos, images in, 160
    product descriptions for, 159–160,
        175–176
    reach of, 154
    resources and information on, 162
    sales amounts generated by, 163
    sales tracking software in, 157, 157!
    Shopify, in creating online stores, 155
    shopping cart system for, 161
    social media and, 163, 164–174

target customers for, 163
tips for building, 158–163
Online sourcing platforms, 80–85
Open to buy (OTB) planning, 77, 93, 94
Operational procedures, 19, 57
Opportunist entrepreneurs, 9
Orders placed at trade shows, 77–79
Outdoor Retailer Show, 70
Outside sources of information/support,
    6–7, 21–37

Parker, Harriet, 24
Paying employees, 57
Payment card industry (PCI)
    compliance, 190
Payment options, online store, 161–162
Peaceful Parlour, 13
Pennsylvania Retailers' Association, 36
Petflow.com, 165
PGA Show, 43
Philosophy, company, 56
Photos, images, online store, 160
Picard, Curtis, 26–27
Picasso, Pablo, 9
Pinterest, 144, 171, 208, 218
PlasticResource.com, 48
Point-of-sale (POS) areas, 121
Point-of-sale (POS) date, 15
Point-of-sales (POS) systems/
    technology, 47, 148, 99–102, 123–126,
    190, 191–194, 210. *See also* Inventory
    management
Premier Packaging, 139, 147, 202, 213
Prescott, Jason, xvii, xix, 68, 85,
    200–202
Press releases, 133, 135–137
Pricing, 90–95
Product descriptions, online store,
    159–160, 175–176
Profit, retail math basics, 90–95
Publications, xv, xvii, 31, 67
Publicity, 7, 134. *See also* Marketing

Quotes and price comparison, sourcing,
    66–67

Radio, 124
Ralish, Shari, 13, 113
Ralph Lauren, xiii

Reed Expositions, 44, 213
Resource listing, 205–218
Retail Adventures Blog, 213
Retail Association of Maine, 26, 36
Retail Association of Nevada, 36
Retail Council of New York State, 36
Retail Jewelers Organization, 32
Retail Merchants Association of New
   Hampshire, 36
Retail Merchants of Hawaii, 36
Retail Minded, xvi, 29, 69, 143, 210,
   214, 218
   conferences by, 33
   Partner Program in, xviii, 31
Retail Minded Magazine, xvii–xviii
Retail Radio, 124, 147, 214
Retail TouchPoints, 167, 172–173, 214
Retailers Association of Massachusetts,
   36
RetailMAVENS, 90, 102, 117, 214
Return on investment, 93
Return policies, 46
Review sites, 97
Reyhle, Nicole Leinbach, 202
Rhode Island Retail Federation, 36
Rice, Jama, 27
Richelson, Jason, 126, 190
Robbins, Tony, 21
Rodgers, Courtney, 144, 159
Rowsell, Vaughn, 99–102, 123, 124, 192

Sale section, 121–122
Sales tracking software, online stores,
   157, 157
Scheduling, 57
SCORE, 33
Search engines, 80
Searching for products online, 80
Sears, xiii, 164
Seasonal employees, 7
Security, 58
Sell through, 93, 117
Selling, 107–131
   cross-merchandising techniques in,
      122
   displays for inventory, 117–123
   e-commerce statistics and, 145
   engaging the senses in, 128–131
   immediate-right zone in, 120

mobile commerce and, 126–128
point of sale (POS) areas and, 121
sale section in, 121–122
sound to enhance buying experience
   and, 124
staples vs. statements in, 122–123
store calendar and, 109–111
store stoppers in, 120–121
technology for, 123–126
Selling your store, 197–200
Shift Your Shopping program, 182, 184,
   185, 214
Shipping, 65
online store, 162–163
Shipwire, 173, 215
Shop Indie Retail, 215
Shop Small campaign, 183–185, 215–216
Shop-local initiatives, 177–188
   American Independent Business
      Alliance (AMIBA) and, 178–182,
      185
   BALLE calculators and, 182
   Business Alliance for Local Living
      Economies (BALLE) and,
      181–182, 185
   buy-local campaigns and, 178–182
   charity events and, 185–186
   Institute for Local Self-Reliance
      and, 185
   Shift Your Shopping program and,
      182, 184, 185
   Shop Small campaign and, 183–185
   Small Business Saturday campaign
      and, 183–185
   starting your own campaign for,
      186–188
Shopify, 145, 147, 154, 155, 162, 173, 202,
   215
ShopKeep, 126, 190, 215
Shopping cart systems, online store, 161
Sierra Pacific Crafts, 216
Sight, engaging the senses in selling,
   128–129
Signage, 3, 147
Silver Barn, The, 12, 133–134
SixDegrees.org, 215
SkipMcGrath.com, 165
Small and medium-sized enterprises
   (SMEs), 216

Small Business Administration (SBA), 217

Small Business Development Centers (SBDC), 24, 206, 217

Small Business Saturday campaign, 183–185

Smart Retailer, xvii

SmartSign, 147

Smell, engaging the senses in selling, 130

Smile: Sell More with Amazing Customer Service (Manecke), 54

SnapRetail, 110–111, 138, 140, 141, 142, 143, 147, 167, 168, 170, 173, 202, 216

Sobbott, Susan, 183

Social media, 16, 45, 123, 140, 153, 163, 164–174, 201
  70-20-10 rule in, 170
  Boutique Window and, 171
  Facebook in, 166, 171
  finding right channel in, 170–171
  Google+ in, 171
  Instagram in, 171
  Pinterest in, 171
  resources and information for, 172
  sales generated through, 164
  SnapRetail offering in, 168
  time requirements to participate in, 170
  Twitter in, 171
  use of, by merchants, 167
  "voice" in, 169

Society of American Florists, 32

Software as a service (SAAS), 193

Sound to enhance buying experience, 124

Sound, engaging the senses in selling, 129–130

Source Direct, 62

Sourcing, 61–87
  budgeting for, 68
  Business-to-Business (B2B) sourcing platforms for, 80–85
  important points to remember in, 64
  international, 64–65, 66
  Internet for, 66
  networking for, 67
  online platforms for, 80–85
  publications about, 67
  quotes and price comparison in, 66–67
  resources and information on, 69
  retailer benefits of, 62–69
  search engines to locate products in, 80
  trends in, 67–68
  U.S. Customs regulations and, 65
  unexpected issues in, 68

SourcingJournalOnline.com, 67, 69

South Carolina Retail Association, 36

South Dakota Retailers Association, 36

Specialist entrepreneurs, 9

Specialty Toy Industry, 32

Square, SquareUp.com., 202, 216

Staff. *See* employees and staff

Standing out among other retailers, 3–7

Staples, 153

Staples vs. statements displays, 122–123

Starbucks, 191

State Chamber of Oklahoma, xviii

State-level retail associations, 25–37

Stella Blue Design, 4

Stock to sales ratio, 93

Stock-keeping unit (SKU) numbers, 104

STOPfakes, 216

Stoppers, store stoppers, 120–121

Store calendar, 109–111

Store contact information, 56, 161

Store hours, 49, 56

Store Specialty Services, 216

Store stoppers as, 120–121

Store traditions, 50

Store window, 119

Story of your store, 39–58

Strategic alignment, 108

Sumner Communications, Inc., 195

Suppliers, 66–67. *See also* Sourcing

Supporting other local businesses, 17

Surveys, 45

Sutton, Cynthia, 12, 133–134, 138, 146

Target, 165

Targeting customers, 7, 15, 163

Tarsus Group, 44, 217

Taste, engaging the senses in selling, 130–131

Taxes, 211

Technology, 123–126, 190–191. *See also*
    Point of sales (POS)
    future beyond, 194
Teele, Suzy, 138, 140, 141, 167, 170
Tennessee Retail Association, 37
Termination of employees, 57
Texas Retailers Association, 37
The Limited, xiii
Things Remembered, xiii
Thomasnet.com, 81
Tiffany, 139
TopTenWholesale.com, xvii, 62, 67, 69,
    81, 83–85, 218
Touch, engaging the senses in selling,
    129
Trade Show Exhibitors Association
    (TSEA), 217
Trade shows, 17, 29, 41–44, 61, 66, 67,
    70, 71–77
    educational opportunities of, 82
    guide to, 43
    open-to-buy (OTB) budget in, 77
    orders placed at, 77–79
    preparing to attend, 86–87
    tips for attending, 78
Trade-specific organizations, 27
Trademark The Spot, 217
Tradeology, 69
Traditions, store, 50
Training employees and yourself, 16–17,
    20, 74–75
Travel discounts, 31
Trends, 30, 67
TripAdvisor, 201
Tripar International, 147–148, 217
Twitter, xvi, 144, 171, 183, 201, 208, 218

U.S. Customs regulations, 65
U.S. National Association of
    Manufacturers, 69
U.S. Patent and Trademark Office
    (USPTO), 217
U.S. Small Business Administration
    (SBA), 217
Unique image, in online retail, 158–159

Unique traits of your store, 44–58
Utah Retail Merchants Association, 37

Vend, 99–102, 123, 148, 192, 202, 218
Vendors, 6, 17, 41, 58, 74, 93
    maintained markup (MMU) and, 94
Vermont Retail Association, 37
Via Trading, 219
Vine, 174, 218
VIP customer care, 47–48
Virginia Retail Merchants Association, 37
"Voice," in social media, 169

Wagner, Cathy, 90, 92, 102, 117, 118, 214
Wagner, Paul, 214
Walmart, 153, 165, 191, 201
Washington Mutual, 108
Washington Retail Association, 37
Waubonsee Community College, 24
Websites, 7. *See also* Online presence/
    Online stores
West Virginia Retailers Association, 37
Western Retailer, xvii
WeWear.org., 206
Wholesale 101: A Guide to… (Prescott), 68
Wholesale District in Los Angeles,
    The, 73
Wholesale markets, 66
Wholesale Minded Magazine, 218
WholesaleCrafts.com, 81, 218
Wholesalers, xvii, 62, 67, 69–71, 81, 83,
    218
    marts and buying districts for, 73
Window displays, 3, 119
Windows POS systems, 190
Wirtz, Ella, 171
Wishpond, 173–174, 218
Women's Wear Daily, xv
World Market Center, 73
Wyoming Retail Association, 37

Yahoo, 80
Yelp.com, 97, 201

Zigler, Zig, 133

About the Authors

Nicole Leinbach Reyhle is an experienced retail and wholesale professional with a passion for small businesses. After years of holding both regional and national management roles for companies including Nordstrom, Adidas America, Sears, and Franco Sarto Footwear, Reyhle founded Retail Minded in 2007 to support independent retailers throughout the world.

Intended to help individual business owners thrive, Retail Minded delivers valuable news, education, and support specific to independent merchants. Since 2011, Reyhle has also supported the retail and small business community through her quarterly publication, *Retail Minded* magazine, as well as through the Retail Minded Partner Program, which affiliates with many associations and organizations in an effort to deliver retail education and support to merchants from all sectors.

Reyhle's online website, RetailMinded.com, has over 1,500 articles specific to retail education for small businesses, and Reyhle has written and published over 500 articles in a variety of other publications as well. A frequent speaker at both national and international events, Reyhle is the cofounder of the Independent Retailer Conference, which is committed to delivering quality education to merchants with one to ten stores. Reyhle is active in a variety of retail- and small business-focused advisory boards throughout the United States and continuously works to stay engaged in retail trends, research, and news.

Reyhle serves as a spokesperson and advisor for Small Business Saturday, a nationally recognized day occuring the Saturday after Thanksgiving that supports small businesses. American Express is a founding partner of Small Business Saturday. Reyhle has been an adjunct instructor at Columbia College Chicago since 2004, teaching various retail and business courses.

Reyhle resides in the Chicago area with her husband, their two young children, and their Weimaraner. Follow Reyhle on Twitter at @RetailMinded and on Facebook at Facebook .com/RetailMinded.

Jason A. Prescott, CEO of JP Communications Inc., directs a network of global trade platforms used for sourcing products by millions of businesses and entrepreneurs. Anchored by TopTenWholesale.com and Manufacturer.com, over 2,000,000 manufacturers, wholesalers, importers, retailers, and product resellers belong to the JPC Inc. trade platforms. Jason recently published his first book, *Wholesale 101: A Guide to Product Sourcing for Entrepreneurs and Small Business Owners* (McGraw-Hill, 2013). Prescott spearheaded the acquisition of Manufacturer.com from a group of Chinese nationals and foreign investors in 2009; JP Communications Inc. operates in China under Hangzhou Flat World Sourcing LTD.

Prescott is a pioneer in business-to-business online trade platforms. JP Communications' trade platforms are partnered with industry trade show giants: Sourcing at Magic, ASD, the Off Price Show, Internet Retailer, and the National Hardware Show, and he has given presentations at Search Engine Strategies, SIPPA, SANDIOS, ASD Trade Shows, Sourcing at Magic, and the San Diego Software Council. Prescott authored one of the first search marketing courses for the Search Engine Marketing Professionals Organization and was on SEMPO's Education Committee. Besides presentations and consulting, Prescott has written articles on business and technology appearing in *B2B Online, OMMA, IMediaConnection, CEO* magazine, and Entrepreneur Online. He has also been cited in *Inc.* magazine, *BusinessWeek*, and Forbes Online.

TopTenWholesale was named #1 in Fast Growth Awards (2008) by bizSanDiego and ranked in the Top 20 for Technology awards sponsored by the San Diego *Business Journal*. Prescott was named in the Top 40 Entrepreneurs Under 40 list in 2007 by San Diego's *Metropolitan* magazine and was recognized for Outstanding Emerging Business of the Year by the San Diego Chamber of Commerce.

Prescott is a graduate of Western Connecticut State University and currently lives in Los Angeles, California.

CPSIA information can be obtained at www.ICGtesting.com
Printed in the USA
BVOW02s2037180815

413941BV00008B/122/P

9 780071 840149